The Great God Baseball

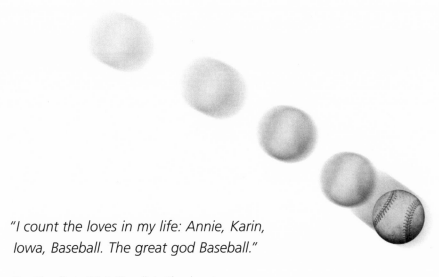

"*I count the loves in my life: Annie, Karin, Iowa, Baseball. The great god Baseball.*"

Ray Kinsella in W. P. Kinsella's *Shoeless Joe*

Sports and Religion

A series edited by Joseph Price

This series explores the academic study of the connection of religion and sports. The series will include books that examine sports through various disciplines and cultural forms (literature, history, music, poetry, among others) and that consider how sports challenge, inspire, or function as religion.

Titles

Joseph L. Price, ed., *From Season to Season: Sports as American Religion*

Allen Hye, *The Great God Baseball: Religion in Modern Baseball Fiction*

Robert J. Higgs and Michael C. Braswell, *An Unholy Alliance: The Sacred and Modern Sports* (Fall 2004)

Religion in Modern Baseball Fiction

Allen E. Hye

MERCER UNIVERSITY PRESS | MACON, GEORGIA | 2004

ISBN 0-86554-931-X
0-86554-939-7
MUP/H675P288

© 2004 Mercer University Press
1400 Coleman Avenue
Macon, Georgia 31207

First Edition.

Book design by Burt & Burt Studio

∞The paper used in this publication meets the minimum requirements
of American National Standard for Information Sciences—
Permanence of Paper for Printed Library Materials, ANSI Z39.48-1992.

Library of Congress Cataloging-in-Publication Data

CIP data are available from the Library of Congress

Contents

Spring Training: Introduction *1*

Pre-Game Show: Brief Overview of Baseball Fiction and Criticism *13*

Innings:

1 Douglass Wallop,

  The Year the Yankees Lost the Pennant (1954) *21*

2 James F. Donohue, *Spitballs & Holy Water* (1977) *33*

3 Jerome Charyn, *The Seventh Babe* (1979) *45*

4 W. P. Kinsella, *Shoeless Joe* (1982) *59*

5 Eric Rolfe Greenberg, *The Celebrant* (1983) *77*

6 Nancy Willard, *Things Invisible to See* (1984) *89*

7 W. P. Kinsella, *The Iowa Baseball Confederacy* (1986) *107*

8 David James Duncan, *The Brothers K* (1992) *127*

9 Darryl Brock, *Havana Heat* (2000) *147*

Conclusion *165*

Extra Innings: Appendix *169*

 Thumbnail Sketches of Other Works *169*

 Religious and Baseball Art *172*

 All-Religious Name Baseball Club *175*

 Baseball in the Bible *176*

 Two Tall Tales *177*

 Quiz on "Religion as Baseball" *178*

 Quotable Quotes *180*

 Answers to Quiz *182*

Works Cited *183*

Index *189*

This book is dedicated to the good people listed in the Acknowledgments, who in various ways have enriched my lifelong relationship to baseball, and who know better than I can express here what they have meant to this book, my career, and my life.

Acknowledgments

Sincere thanks go to my wife, Roberta, #2 in the Fan Rating System but #1 in my heart, for a thorough reading of the manuscript and constant encouragement throughout the project;

My daughter, Courtney, who ducked to let me catch my first major league ball after 40 years of trying;

My son, Carsten, for years of backyard catches and baseball road trips;

My brother, Paul, for putting up with more baseball talk than a casual fan should have to endure;

Pete Petreman, who, when the project was in its infancy, inspired me to continue with a little note, "I believe in this book," and for his many helpful suggestions for the manuscript;

Writers W. P. Kinsella and James F. Donohue, for stimulating conversation about the creative process behind their novels;

Hol Hollopeter and George Baldwin, two terrific coaches, for the many hours—nay, years—they devoted to teaching us baseball, teamwork, and discipline from Little League through high school;

Greg Anderson, for getting the ball rolling by insisting that I read *Shoeless Joe;*

Gary Nuhn, sportswriter extraordinaire and the Commish, for introducing me to fantasy baseball, and my brother-in-law Rob Tracy, for sharing tips and strategy that made my team respectable;

PCA colleagues Joe Price, Doug Noverr, and Larry Ziewacz, for their encouragement as I developed papers on religion in baseball fiction;

SABR colleagues Peter Bjarkman, Gary Land, and Richard Gaughran, who shared much of their research on baseball history and literature, and Jack Carlson, Dave Fitzsimmons, and John Schleppi, the heart of the order in Dayton's SABR chapter;

Helen and the late Richard L. Miller, for inviting me to share in their college course on baseball and their friendship;

Kathie Hormby, wife of my cousin David, mother of Tom, and inspiration to thousands, for her courageous, ongoing battle against Lou Gehrig's disease, her love of baseball and the Dodgers, and her wit: "If I have to die, at least it has something to do with baseball."

Marc Jolley and his colleagues at Mercer University Press, for their interest in my work and assistance with bringing it to fruition.

Spring Training: Introduction

If I were not a Christian, I would worship baseball.
The Reverend Dr. Greg Anderson

"*Baseball?* You're going to teach an honor's class on *baseball?*" Such was the reaction—along with laughter—when we first announced our upcoming team-taught course at Wright State University on baseball and American society. My colleagues and I pointed to the cultural significance of the national pastime and compared our baseball course with what are often called music or art appreciation courses—they are all taught by people who really *love* their subject and want to inculcate in the students, if not love, at least an increased understanding and appreciation of it. Despite our course's success and the fact that the honors program wanted it repeated, skeptics still remained; old biases die hard.

Likewise, when I say I give conference papers and write articles on baseball fiction, people are often incredulous. Of course, that could be because

my primary academic identity is as a professor of German, but I suspect it is more that most casual fans and readers still associate baseball with juvenile literature or hokey films. Understandably so, for I too grew up on Zane Grey and Clair Bee novels and only later discovered the scintillating world of what is often called "adult baseball fiction." Since then I have felt something of a calling to minister to the skeptics and have been gratified by their surprise and delight at encountering W. P. Kinsella, Eric Rolfe Greenberg, and others.

To illustrate the depth of first-rate baseball literature, I am fond of quoting Lawrence Ritter's remark in his classic oral history, *The Glory of Their Times*:

> What is *Moby Dick* about? Is it a book about whaling in the nineteenth century? Indeed it is. It probably contains more information on the subject than any learned treatise written before or since. Nevertheless, any schoolboy knows that *Moby Dick* is not really about whaling. It is about man's hopes, his struggles, his triumphs, and his failures. It is about trying to attain the unattainable—and sometimes making it. And, on its own terms, that is also what this book is about (xv)

Ritter's words also hold true for baseball's best novels—they are not *really* about baseball but about life:[1] our dreams and fears, success and failure, obsessions and loves, family and solitude, of attaining, as Kinsella is wont to say, "our heart's desire." They are also about us as Americans, and

---

[1] Some have made the case that one should not apologize for writing about baseball nor pretend that these novels are not about the game. Perhaps one could say that they are not "only" about baseball. As David Carkeet has quipped, "The only book that is about baseball and nothing else is the rule book" (Horvath and Palmer 186).

in them we learn much about our history and ourselves. Indeed, at least one honors student commented that her course highlight was an enhanced understanding of American history.[2]

Genesis and Epiphany

"Allen, I know you're very busy at work, but you simply *have* to read this book." These insistent words by my good friend Greg Anderson as he thrust Kinsella's classic, *Shoeless Joe*, into my hand were the genesis of my acquaintance with adult baseball fiction. The novel, with its whimsical treatment of serious life issues, so flabbergasted me that I wanted to share it with others, *at once!* After reviewing it for our small campus baseball magazine, *The Pine Tar Review*, I soon found other outlets for my new passion: the Society for American Baseball Research (SABR) and the Popular Culture Association (PCA), where I encountered many like-minded academics who encouraged my research and writing on the novels that are the subject of this study.

Delving more into modern baseball fiction, I realized—in something of an epiphany—that with each new book and paper I gravitated to a single, prominent theme, namely religion. Since Americans are essentially a religious people, it is not surprising that this is also a major element in novels about our national pastime, one that should not be ignored. If some readers are puzzled or put off by the reference to religion, they need not be, for

---

[2] The symbiotic relationship between baseball and American history was impressively developed in a popular course offered by the late Richard L. Miller at the University of Cincinnati. More recently, Jules Tygiel has written a book of essays on this topic, *Past Time: Baseball as History*, of which he explains, "If there is a unifying theme in these chapters, it is that, while the game of baseball itself has changed minimally since its origins, the context and format in which Americans have absorbed and appreciated the game have dramatically shifted" (x). That context can be better grasped through a familiarity with the baseball fiction we are discussing here.

just as baseball fiction is not *juvenile* but *adult*, so its religious themes are not elementary Sunday school lessons but rich slices of the human—and specifically American—experience.

Proclaiming the Gospel, or Why I Wrote This Book

I've often said that had I not been a professor, I may have become a librarian, for I love books and love telling people about them, in this case to proclaim the word of a body of outstanding, underappreciated fiction. For readers who make no association between baseball and good literature, this means introducing them to the modern classics of Kinsella and others; and for those who *do* know the major works, it involves calling to their attention the lesser known nuggets of James Donohue, Nancy Willard, and others. Put another way, I'd like to introduce baseball to book fans and books to baseball fans.[3] I vividly recall the reaction offered by our department chair—an *un*-fan if ever there was one—when I arranged an appearance by W. P. Kinsella on our campus. My colleague attended the reading only out of a sense of duty, but afterward she registered grudging approval: "At last I understand why this 'baseball stuff' has attracted so much attention."

Another way of expressing my missionary call to baseball fiction is to consider the fan rating system with which we had so much fun at the beginning of the inaugural honors seminar on baseball. I ranked the intensity of a fan's interest and knowledge on a scale from 1 to 7 as follows:

---

[3] Baseball people are not generally known for being avid readers. Of Hall of Fame manager Sparky Anderson and others with ghostwritten autobiographies, it is said, "He is the only guy I know who's written more books than he's read."

(1) *My grandmother*—I would try to explain the game to her by drawing charts and showing her pictures, but nothing worked. She would smile sweetly and thank me for trying, but it never took.

(2) *My wife*—She is perfectly capable of understanding the game but doesn't care to. Offers of dinner, good seats, and the company of friends still won't get her to the park…or me to first base.

(3) *Non-fan*—Will attend games for food, fellowship, fresh air, or fireworks; may neither know the score nor care who won.

(4) *Casual fan*—Roots for the home team; knows the basic rules and the names of a few key players; may like the game without being able to articulate why.

(5) *Knowledgeable fan*—Knows the import of the game in question and other games going on in the league; familiar with more sophisticated strategy and can identify most key players.

(6) *Serious fan*—Has a sense of history and aesthetics; aware of fine points of the game and appreciates the cultural importance of baseball; probably keeps score.

(7) *Fanatic*—This fan is consumed by stats, trivia, and the minutiae of a favorite team or player, generally at the expense of the virtues of #6. He is a danger to the mental health and stability of himself and his family.[4] If #6 is a wine connoisseur, this guy is a wino. (A favorite example of #7 is our

---

[4] I use extreme language like "danger" only partly tongue-in-cheek. Consider former MLB Commissioner Bart Giamatti's concern that devotion to sport can create cult as well as community: "The cultic dimension of sports—with the attendant fanaticism of some fans, and the complete absorption into the temple such that nothing else obtrudes or matters to many athletes—is dangerous" (56).

WSU colleague who lived and died with the New York Mets and their star pitcher, Tom Seaver. When, driving off on his honeymoon in 1977, he turned on the radio and learned of Seaver's trade to Cincinnati, the misguided professor wailed, "This is the worst day of my life!")

In terms of the rating system, we aimed with our honors course to move the less committed students up a notch or two or—in the case of severe fanatics—bring them back a notch toward sanity and a balanced life. Likewise, I hope with this book to increase the knowledge and appreciation of readers both for the game of baseball and the delightful literature that immortalizes it.

Many of the novels discussed in this study have, until now, had little or no critical analysis, and while a few critics do explore the religious qualities of some novels (especially *Shoeless Joe*), to my knowledge there has been no major study written on this prominent topic. Thus, another aim of my book is to fill gaps in existing scholarship. At the same time, although the individual chapters are literary analyses, they are *not* for scholars and literary critics only. I fervently hope the enthusiasm that prompted me to write this book will be so evident that people will want to *read*—not just read *about*—the terrific works discussed in it.

Baseball is like church—many attend but few understand.
Wes Westrum

The old Giants catcher and manager delivered his quip long before the conception of this book, but it is as if he created it especially for us. Because literature can be as difficult to understand as baseball and religion, I will endeavor in the following ways to make the baseball novels more accessible to casual as well as serious readers, fans and non-fans alike:

(1) The *inclusion* of good, lesser-known works as well as classics. Both the quality of the novels and the quantity of religious references determine their coverage here. Works with fewer but more artfully done religious references will merit greater coverage than those with an obvious but less compelling treatment of religion.

(2) Discussion of the novels in *chronological order* to facilitate an understanding of the development of baseball fiction over the last five decades.

(3) *Detective work* accomplished by author interviews, study of theoretical writings, and serendipity. These elements take the reader further behind the scenes to appreciate the emergence of a new work.

(4) The *key motifs* of each work, which are highlighted to point back to previous works and ahead to subsequent ones. Analysis of striking elements of *narrative structure* makes the novel more accessible to the reader. Many *cross-references* illustrate the ongoing exchange between authors and help the reader locate the works in a literary context.

(5) An *appendix* called "Extra Innings," which, in addition to a list of works cited, includes (a) thumbnail sketches of baseball fiction that, while worthy of mention, doesn't contain enough material on our topic to warrant its own chapter; and (b) a gallery of many varied comparisons of baseball to religion—lists, cartoons, photos, humorous stories, and quotes. These materials not only provide an amusing complement to the essays, but

they also demonstrate how pervasive our society's sense of baseball is as a kind of civil religion.

Baseball is more than a game to me—it's a religion.
Hall of Fame umpire Bill Klem

What is it about baseball that led Bill Klem to call it a religion and inspired so many novelists to ascribe religious qualities to the game? Perhaps it is an innate understanding that the game itself possesses religious character in its familiar ritual and sense of sacred space. Even casual fans may recognize a certain ritualistic quality to baseball. The long season, with its almost daily games, weaves baseball into the fabric of American life. Players and the announcers who bring them into our homes and cars become like old, trusted friends, and our daily routine is infused with the games' routine or ritual: pre-game show, manicured infield, lineups, national anthem, "Play ball," three-up-three-down, colorful commercials, flashing signs, strategy, seventh-inning stretch, "Take Me Out to the Ballgame," clutch hit, key strikeout, post-game show, box score. As Hall of Fame manager Earl Weaver reminds us, "This ain't a football game. We do this every day."[5]

Upon these daily rituals of baseball in our lives are superimposed the more formal rites that express the game's religious qualities. Although not deliberately created as religious expression, they nonetheless illustrate how

[5] Cited in Thomas Boswell, *How Life Imitates the World Series*, 5.

the complex and subtle game inspires, even if subconsciously, the need to express what theologian Frederick Streng calls "the ultimate dimension,…that to which one gives one's loyalty as the pervading character of life" (5),[6] which creates the civil religion called baseball. Writers such as Thomas Boswell and David Chidester, playing off Annie Savoy's famous opening quote in the movie *Bull Durham*, have written about "The Church of Baseball," while Thomas F. Dailey, OSFS, has made a formal study of "The Religious Power of Our National Pastime."

Another theologian, Joseph L. Price, has analyzed the mythic and religious nature of baseball ritual within the game itself—the groundskeepers' "ritual of consecration" in preparing the field, the ball as "sacred object" introduced only by an umpire or a dignitary "tossing out the first ball"—and cites several examples of how the ritual becomes established religion:

> In addition to its religious affections for rules, baseball has its temples—its stadiums—where the rites are performed—and its shrines—like the Hall of Fame…[with] its cult of saints, its superheroes of bygone years…. Baseball, like religions, also has its relics, its tangible artifacts that help to call to mind the journeys to the games and the contact with the heroes…. Like many religions, baseball has its sacred texts—the official tables of statistics and the official publications from yearbooks to the fans' weekly tract, the *Sporting News*, which for years bore the subtitle, "The Baseball Bible." Baseball also has its high priests, like All-Star pitchers and Cy Young Award winners, and its true believers, like the most faithful fans who, typified by

[6] For Streng, the devotion of Umpire Klem and several of baseball's literary characters qualifies as religious. The fact that the events "may occur outside of traditional religious life makes them no less 'ultimate' for those who experience them" (5).

Cubs' devotees, never give up even when hope has become unreasonable. Like some religions, baseball identifies its sins by calculating and tabulating errors for fielders, strike outs for batters, and walks, balks, and hit batters for pitchers. Finally, baseball has its own liturgical calendar—its own list of holy days or holidays that begins with the festive "new year" celebrations of Opening Day...and concludes with the high holidays of the divisional playoffs and World Series (63-64).

Hallowed Ground

Price sees in baseball's spatial configuration the subconscious manifestation of the Greek omphalos myth, the myth of the sacred, elevated center, with "the pitcher's mound as cosmic mountain" (61-76), while several works—e.g., *The Temple of Baseball, Green Cathedrals,* or Bill Goff's ballpark calendars titled *Hallowed Ground*—convey the idea of the baseball field as a sacred space in which religious ritual is celebrated. And, as we shall see, the ballpark is often a holy place in baseball fiction.

The theologians and novelists are merely documenting that to which countless fans have responded, the almost mystical attraction of a ball field. It arises initially from one's encounter with a park in the midst of a city—the pastoral amid the urban, cool grass as an oasis in the hot, granite desert—or the vision of a field as it emerges through a narrow tunnel or walkway leading to the grandstand. Even today I vividly recall the thrill of seeing my first major league park, Yankee Stadium, my senses filled by the sight of green grass, brown dirt, and white lines, the sounds of the ball against a bat and glove, and the smell and taste of grilling food and splashing drink. Decades later, my first visit to Chicago's Wrigley Field had a similar effect, which I reported to amused friends as "akin to a religious experience." That put me in the good company of Shoeless Joe Jackson, who upon first arriving at Ray Kinsella's cornfield park, asks, "Is this heaven?"

For the three hours or so that a fan is at a ball game, the field indeed becomes like a church, a place of renewal set apart (the meaning of "sacred"), a safe harbor from the storms of life. The late baseball commissioner Bart Giamatti implies this with his posthumously published tribute to the game, *Take Time for Paradise*. "All play," he writes, "aspires to the condition of paradise…. Where it exists, we do not know, although we have always envisioned it as a garden, sometimes on a mountaintop, often on an island, but always as removed, as an enclosed, green space" (42). "It's like my Garden of Eden in the middle of life," states one devoted Cleveland fan. "No matter what else is going wrong, it's always there and everything is all right once I'm inside."[7]

Both real worship and real baseball, rightly done, can have similar restorative effects. Both draw us out of one realm into another, where we are renewed, re-created (in the core sense of "recreation"). This happens because of our individual encounter with the Creator/Spirit of baseball, and is intensified by the fellowship we enjoy with other believers/fans. Eric Rolfe Greenberg wonderfully portrays the crowd dynamics in *The Celebrant*, and in *Shoeless Joe*, Kinsella compares the ability to see the ghostly players with the gift of faith, the spiritual eyes that allow some worshipers to believe while others shake their heads and see nothing. Those who can see, who are attuned to the spiritual blessings of ritual in a sacred space, be it in church or a ballpark, emerge different people.

We have seen examples of how these religious qualities of baseball translate to literature, but let us for a moment consider the authors' stance

---

[7] *USA Today*, 5 August 1993.

toward religion. We must understand that religious themes serve a practical, literary function. The writers are first and foremost storytellers, and they employ what works—if there were no spiritual dimension to their readers' lives, the religious references would likely not connect with them. At the same time, I wish to alert my readers to the fact that the presentation of religious motifs will vary greatly. Some may be mere literary gimmicks, plucking the reader's heartstrings or tweaking the fans' quasi-religious devotion to the game, while other themes may reflect the author's own spiritual situation. Nonbelieving writers may be neutral or critical, respectful or profane. Believers may be Christians or Jews, Protestants or Catholics, monotheists or polytheists, firm in their faith or wavering on the edge. Their use of religious motifs may be purely functional or ornamental, as with the professed atheist W. P. Kinsella, or, as with David James Duncan's work on Seventh Day Adventism, *The Brothers K*, may involve the novelist's encounter with faith.

Finally, like the writers themselves, their work assumes many forms as it both documents and enriches the game of life in which we are all players. Religion in the great baseball novels is both devotion and *parody* of devotion. It illustrates social history and social criticism, family bonds and family tensions. It reflects monotheism and spiritism, scripture and superstition, the temporal and the eternal, redemption and resurrection. The religious dimension in baseball fiction draws us into an encounter with the wonder of life—our society, our national pastime, our imagination, and our sense of spiritual awareness. From our literary encounter we emerge, as if from a church, temple, or ballpark, different, re-created people. I should be most gratified if this book were an agent for the intellectual, spiritual, and emotional renewal offered by the great game and literature of baseball.

Pre-Game Show

Brief Overview of Baseball Fiction and Criticism

The appeal of serious baseball fiction is that it addresses both the eternal qualities of human existence—life and death, love and hate, family and loneliness, fathers and sons, beauty and ugliness—and the social concerns that baseball increasingly raises by virtue of its being our national pastime—our pastoral roots and urban development, immigration and assimilation, racism and integration, war and peace. The theme that has most interested me in these works, and one that necessarily touches on the others, is that of religion. Religious allusions are surprisingly prominent in baseball fiction, even in the works of nonbelievers. They sense the spiritual, timeless qualities of the game and alternately venerate and spoof the almost religious devotion of fans to the game and to their teams and heroes. The oft-quoted Jacques Barzun has stated that to understand America one must know baseball, and the same can be said of religion, for America from its beginning has been a distinctly religious land. Thus, it is no surprise that

our nation's religious roots and national pastime intersect so prominently in its literature.

Yet this has not always been the case, as chroniclers of baseball fiction such as Andy McCue—whose "Modest History of Baseball Fiction" (the first chapter of *Baseball by the Books*) I will highlight here—have demonstrated. For decades, beginning in 1884 with "the first novel that was almost completely devoted to baseball" (1), Noah Brooks's *Our Base Ball Club and How It Won the Championship*, baseball fiction was dominated by, and relegated to, juvenile literature. Affordable, small-format books about American history and the Wild West, commonly called dime novels, extended their reach to baseball. The year 1896 brought Gilbert Patten's hugely popular and widely imitated Frank Merriwell series, written under the name of Burt L. Standish and published by Street & Smith in the *Tip Top Weekly*; however, with the development of more efficient publishing techniques in the early twentieth century, dime novels were converted into books. Edward Stratemeyer, the foremost purveyor of inexpensive books for young readers, initiated the popular series about Baseball Joe, the first professional star in juvenile fiction. Using a world of pseudonyms and a stable of other writers, he created the so-called Stratemeyer Syndicate that lasted well beyond his death and produced many other series, including Nancy Drew mysteries and the Hardy Boys.

Most baseball fiction showed heroes of social values triumphing over life's adversities and over those who would not conform to the norm. As McCue points out, it was John Tunis, writing during and after World War II, who first criticized society more than the individual and created characters in shades of gray, not just black or white. Later juvenile fiction addressed more contemporary topics (Little League, racial and gender integration), but the number of series dwindled until returning on a small scale in the 1990s.

But what of *adult* baseball fiction? Throughout the decades we have outlined, only two significant books of baseball fiction were created for the adult reader: Ring Lardner's *You Know Me Al* (1916), comprised of humorous letters from a Chicago White Sox player to a friend, and Heywood Broun's *The Sun Field* (1923), a story of love and baseball narrated by a former sportswriter. Baseball was not considered a fit topic for works of literary rank and it was not until the early 1950s that the breakthrough came, with Bernard Malamud's *The Natural* (1952) and Mark Harris's *The Southpaw* (1953), the latter being the first of four novels "written" and narrated by Henry "Author" Wiggen, a fictional New York pitcher. These novels legitimized baseball as a serious subject in American literature. They broke open the door for the works covered in our study and for the wealth of fine baseball novels that appeared in the second half of the twentieth century. The Harris books have no significant religious dimension and are not cited in the following analyses, but Malamud's classic is a touchstone for our novels and merits mention here in something of a prelude to the overall study of religion in baseball fiction.

The Natural

For much of the writing of this study, Malamud's novel held down the lead-off spot in our literary lineup. It is, after all, the godfather of modern baseball fiction and arguably the most cited, studied, or imitated work of its kind. (In my opinion, only W. P. Kinsella's *Shoeless Joe* rates comparable consideration as the most influential novel in the field and has attracted as much scholarly attention.) However, in limiting my lineup to nine novels, I decided to "bench" *The Natural* for two reasons. First, it doesn't have the distinct religious elements that characterize the other works. Only the broadest interpretation of "religious" would include the novel's allusions to classical mythology and the legends of medieval Christian society, and such a potentially forced reading would, I fear, strain the fabric of the chapter. Second, so much has already been written about *The Natural* that trying to navigate the existing secondary literature and produce a fresh perspective would also risk cramping the writer's and reader's style. Nonetheless, because of its significance for the novels we will discuss, several of which allude to *The Natural*, I wish to orient my reader to the key features of the book and prominent interpretations of it.

The novel's protagonist, Roy Hobbs, is "natural" in two senses of the word: a phenomenal baseball talent, and a naïve country boy. On his way to Chicago for a major league tryout, he shows promise by striking out baseball's reigning slugger, "The Whammer," at a train stop, thereby catching the eye of a femme fatale called Harriet Bird. When they arrive in the big city, she lures Roy to her hotel room and shoots him.

After many years out of the game, Hobbs returns to baseball as an unknown left fielder, becoming a sensation once he breaks into the lineup of the floundering New York Knights. As he resurrects the Knights, Roy becomes involved with two different women: Memo Paris, seductive niece of the team's manager, Pop Fisher, and Iris Lemon, a wholesome, nurturing mother. While Memo drains Roy of his vitality, which leads to a prolonged batting slump, Iris supports and encourages him. As the resurgent Knights approach a playoff for the pennant, Roy accepts a bribe to throw the game. Learning that Iris is expecting his child, he decides too late to play to win, strikes out in disgrace, and faces probable banishment from baseball. "He thought, I never did learn anything out of my past life, and now I have to suffer again" (236).

The Natural is an amazing novel, rife with symbols and textured with layers of mythic allusions that afford various readings, and overlaid on a patchwork quilt of American culture. While the book is unrealistic, dream-like, and symbolic, the squares of the quilt are based on real events and personages from baseball history. No fewer than ten clear historic parallels can be drawn, including the legendary Babe Ruth; Shoeless Joe Jackson, banned from baseball with seven teammates on the 1919 Chicago White Sox; and Eddie Waitkus, shot in 1949 by a deranged woman in a hotel room.

The Natural is not renowned as a book that accurately portrays base-ball, but it uses the game as a framework of a dynamic story with layers of mythic allusions. Scholarship has outlined four prominent readings of the novel:

• ancient myth, ritual, and archetypes, especially of C. G. Jung;

• classical mythology, especially of Homer;

• Arthurian legend, particularly of Percival and the Grail quest;

• modern America, especially the history and ritual of baseball in the aftermath of the 1919 Black Sox scandal.

There is so much more that could be—and has been—said about *The Natural*. For our purposes, this must suffice as an orientation point for the chapter studies to follow, many of which display a kinship to Malamud's work, and all of which are in some way indebted to its pioneering role in the history of baseball fiction.

Critical Studies of Baseball Fiction

Before we begin our work-by-work consideration of religion in baseball fiction, I wish to comment briefly on existing scholarly works that go far beyond the above outline of the genre and of its pioneering exemplar.

Those who wish to read more about *The Natural* will have many fine resources to consult; as mentioned, with the possible exception of W. P. Kinsella, there may be more secondary literature on Malamud and his book than any other. I found the commentary by Sheldon J. Hershinow, Earl R. Wasserman, Sidney Richman, and Kevin Thomas Curtin (the latter interpreting the novel and the film adaptation in light of Homer's *Iliad* and *Odyssey*) to be helpful. An article by Eric Solomon makes Malamud and Harris the starting point for an excellent overview of what he calls Jewish baseball fiction, including two other novels discussed here, *The Celebrant* and *The Seventh Babe*; the latter Solomon examines in detail as a "Jewish-Black baseball novel" (49).

Peter Bjarkman's anthology introduction and several rather recent monographs by Cordelia Candelaria, John Lauricella, David McGimpsey, Deeanne Westbrook (writing about baseball and myth), Richard Peterson, and Timothy Morris deserve mention here as examples of a growing scholarly interest in baseball fiction. Some have entire sections or even chapters on the works we discuss here; others make several shorter references to the novels in the context of the various themes covered in the study. In particular, a few chapters by Peterson and Morris offer substantial overviews of modern baseball fiction, and Morris maintains a fine online bibliography of baseball fiction. Mike Shannon's book with four-to-six-page summaries of and commentary on "100 of the Best Baseball Books" is a most useful reference tool. Editors Christopher H. Evans's and William R. Herzog's collection of essays on "Baseball, Religion, and American Culture" analyzes the cultural soil from which baseball fiction arises. These and many other secondary works listed in the works cited stand ready to take readers farther into the world of baseball writing. For now, let us throw out the first pitch and begin our nine innings with the great god Baseball.

Inning 1:

The Place of *The Year the Yankees Lost the Pennant* in Modern Baseball Fiction

Forget the 111 victories of the 1954 Cleveland Indians! Instead, it is 21 July 1958, and the hated Yankees are charging relentlessly toward their tenth consecutive pennant when a frustrated middle-aged Washington Senators fan named Joe Boyd is approached by the Devil with an unimaginable offer: in exchange for his soul, the Devil, named Applegate, will transform him into Joe Hardy, a sensational young outfielder who will lead the Senators to a pennant. Joe agrees, but only with an "escape clause" that he can exercise two months hence, on 21 September. Joe leaves a note for his wife and embarks on his pro career, taking the American League by storm and leading Washington to within a few games of the league-leading Yankees. Questions regarding his background and eligibility convince the baseball commissioner to suspend Joe until a hearing can be held. When through the deceit of Applegate, the hearing extends past the deadline for Joe's

return, it appears that not only is his soul lost, but the pennant as well. Ultimately, with two great plays of his own Joe defeats the Yankees, and with the help of a softhearted femme fatale named Lola, who would like to keep him as her own in the Devil's employ, he strikes a deal for a safe return to his wife.

The author of this delightful fantasy, *The Year the Yankees Lost the Pennant*, was John Douglass Wallop III (1920-1985). A University of Maryland journalism graduate, Wallop was so talented at shorthand that he was commissioned to serve as Dwight Eisenhower's amanuensis for the general's dictated memoir, *Crusade in Europe*. Furthermore, Wallop wrote all of his eleven novels in shorthand, never with a typewriter. *The Year the Yankees Lost the Pennant* was his second novel and revealed what the book's dust jacket hails as the two essential facts about the author: "He is a born storyteller and he is that most forlorn of men, a fan of the Washington American League baseball team." Indeed, as the book progresses, it is amusing to see how the author uses it to take literary revenge on the Yankees for a lifetime of frustration, casting them as evil incarnate, supported by the Devil himself.

Despite positive contemporary reviews, the novel is virtually ignored in the history of modern baseball fiction. To my knowledge, only Deeanne Westbrook in *Ground Rules*, who compares Wallop's hero to Odysseus, and Mike Shannon in *Diamond Classics*, who stresses Wallop's adaptation of the Faust legend, give it any critical attention at all, in two and six pages respectively. Perhaps the novel was buried under the enormous success of its offspring, the musical *Damn Yankees*, which appeared only a year later on Broadway and four years later on film (with Wallop as one of four collaborating playwrights). Perhaps literary critics also underestimate the book because it appeared well before baseball fiction began to be taken seriously.

It was a Book-of-the-Month Club selection with a lighthearted tone and as such relegated to popular, not serious, literature. Wallop's easy manner and smooth writing belie the weighty questions raised by the hero's entanglement with the Devil, threats to his marriage, and salvation.

One aim of this chapter is to consider Mike Shannon's claim that the novel is "one of the most underrated of the great works of baseball literature" (417), and like Shannon I will discuss Wallop's adaptation of the Faust legend as a primary model for the novel. Beyond that, however, I will suggest other literary antecedents and descendants in seeking to place Wallop's work in the context of the superior baseball fiction that developed in the second half of the twentieth century.

Biblical Themes

Although this is not an overtly "religious" novel, there is a plethora of biblical allusions in Wallop's witty text, initially in Applegate's appeal to Joe to be "Moses" to his hometown team, to "lead them out of the wilderness" (19), then in Joe's own thoughts that rationalize his dealings with the Devil. Though recognizing the "evil aspect" (25) of consorting with the Devil, he convinces himself that he is combating a greater evil: "Could an aim so worthy as denying the Yankees a tenth consecutive pennant be evil?" (26). Like Moses, Joe sees himself as "chosen" (26) to fulfill his duty to the people, not the Hebrews but long-suffering Senator fans. His adventure is also "like a crusade. And a crusade, by its very nature, meant glory as well as sacrifice" (26). He justifies his absence as a "sabbatical" from his marriage of thirty years (coincidentally the age at which Jesus began his public ministry). Joe acknowledges that his goal is "to redeem a baseball team" (78), to be a savior, and when the commissioner's hearing appears to go his way, he considers the success: "He had saved the team, saved its victories intact, saved its chance for the pennant, saved it from shame" (199). Immediately, however, Joe is thrust into a dilemma that, as with Christ, requires sacrifice as the cost of being a savior. For the hearing to be a complete success, Joe must undergo a physical examination, and that delay will take him past midnight on 21 September, the point of no return. He formulates his ethical dilemma as follows: "If I make this sacrifice, it is a good thing to do, and therefore I should be saved from Applegate. But if I take the selfish course and run out, I deserve to be doomed forever" (203).

To complete his role as Washington's savior, Joe chooses sacrifice. He surprises the Devil by making a great catch to hold the Yankees at bay in the final, decisive game: "You saved it for us, Joe," says team owner van Buren. "That catch saved it for us. Can you win it for us now, Joe?" (230). He can. Despite being transformed by Applegate back into the middle-aged Joe Boyd in mid-play, the hero manages to slide home with the pennant-winning run. He has saved Washington, but who will save *him*?

The surprising answer is Lola, the once-homely schoolteacher who received physical beauty from the Devil in exchange for her soul. She has fallen in love with Joe and would like to keep him, but she relinquishes him to *his* true love, wife Bess. Lola tricks the gluttonous Applegate by starving him until he agrees to free Joe. She steals his specially-made shoes, and because of his cloven feet, he cannot go out in public to get food. In revenge, Applegate will take away Lola's beauty, so in addition to losing her beloved, she is willing to sacrifice the one thing that makes her life in hell bearable. Happily, Joe is able to recover her beauty by agreeing to remain silent about the true identity of Applegate's new recruit, a television repairman who has assumed the role of Joe Hardy to help the Senators defeat the Dodgers in the World Series.

The biblical references to hell and the Devil in this novel are complemented by images from folklore, such as the Devil's cloven feet and tongue-in-cheek parallels to New York City, which Applegate "found very homelike" (90). The summer heat that wears out baseball players and fans is still cool for Applegate, who in July, accustomed to the heat of hell, wears a topcoat with the lapels turned up. Likewise, when Joe Boyd is transformed into Joe Hardy, he feels "neither heat nor humidity" (42). His contact with the Devil, however, chills him. He feels "fear crawl his spine" (90) from the "soul-clenching thought" (91) of never returning. Hearing Applegate's "oily voice, a mocking voice, heavy with irony," Joe shivers and feels "frightened and suddenly very small" (125). Wallop's literary lampooning of New York takes a final twist near the end of the novel when we learn that Applegate's machinations are expressly to help his beloved Yankees. The plan calls for Joe to fail in his final game as a Senator, allowing New York to win the pennant, then be traded to the Yankees to help them continue their domination. Apparently, this prospect is worse for a diehard Senator fan than hell itself.

Faustian Bargains

The subtle biblical framework and the magical-folkloric qualities of this novel are also common to the story of Faust, the medieval German alchemist who was reputed to have consorted with the Devil in order to increase his scientific powers. Because of Wallop's obvious debt to the Faust theme, especially in its formulation of the "Faustian bargain," it is instructive to consider the two best-known renditions.

The original printed version of the Faust legend appeared in 1587 in Germany as an anonymously published chapbook that has come to be known as the *Faustbuch* (the History of Doctor Johann Faustus). Written in an ostensibly Christian society, it has, according to its lengthy subtitle, the didactic purpose of being "useful and efficacious as a highly essential Christian warning and admonition" (17). The doctor writes a contract, signed in his blood, that calls quid pro quo for a spirit by the name of Mephistopheles (*a* devil, a "servant of the infernal prince," not *the* Devil) to attend to his every wish for exactly twenty-four years. Thereafter, Faust will relinquish to him all that he has, "body, property, flesh, blood, etc." (34). Faust uses his new power egotistically, to experiment with the supernatural and impress his students. When the twenty-four years are up, Faust sincerely regrets his demonic alliance, asks others to pray for him, and hopes that his repentance will suffice to redeem him. There is, however, no assurance that his soul will survive the violent physical death that befalls him in his final night.

The most prominent of many adaptations of this theme is the two-part drama of Germany's greatest poet, Johann Wolfgang von Goethe (1749-1832), who spent about sixty years on it, completing *Faust II* in the year before his death. The biblical framework for Goethe's *Faust* is given in the "Prologue in Heaven," based on the beginning of the book of Job, in which Satan meets with God and the angels of heaven. In Goethe's "Prologue," God grants Mephistopheles permission to approach Faust but cautions that he will not succeed in winning him forever. Believing he can seduce Faust, Mephistopheles presents first a one-sided offer to be his servant, then suggests a pact similar to the one in the *Faustbuch*: I'll serve you here, and when we meet over there, you'll do the same for me (from verses 1656-1659). Rejecting the pact, Faust challenges Mephisto with what he calls a "bet," that the vain spirit cannot satisfy his, Faust's, striving for ultimate knowledge.

He *risks* his soul; he does not *sell* it. In the end, because his striving has never abated, he is welcomed into heaven, much to Mephisto's consternation.

The crucial distinction between the "pact" and "bet" is upheld in *The Year the Yankees Lost the Pennant*, where I believe it is not correct to speak of Joe Boyd "selling" his soul to the Devil. Applegate lets Joe sample the physical prowess of a young superstar and, like Mephisto, hopes for a quick deal with nothing specific said about the terms. Joe, however, probes for details, and when he learns that the arrangement is "forever" and in a place that's "fairly well known," (29) (i.e., hell), he, like Goethe's Faust, rejects the quid pro quo. He insists on an "escape clause," to which Applegate agrees with a limp handshake. Once Joe has joined the Senators ball club, he and Applegate sign a contract to that effect: on 21 September, *and that day only*, two months to the day after they met, Joe has the right to insist on escape from Applegate's grasp and restoration to his former self. Confident that he can outwit the Devil, yet sensing a "chill premonition" (56), Joe signs the contract, which he, like Goethe's Faust, is fortunate to survive.

Parallels to *The Natural*

Just as important a source for Wallop was, I believe, Bernard Malamud's recently published novel of a star-crossed phenomenon, *The Natural*, to which I will make six comparisons. Consider first the outward similarities: an unknown outfielder with no professional credentials appears unannounced before the harried manager of a miserable major league baseball club asking for a chance to play: "Where've you been playing, fella?.... Oh, here and there.... Where is here and there? Well, to be honest, it was mostly sandlot ball, but I can hit a ball quite a distance, I think" (39-40). Joe, like Roy Hobbs before him, overcomes initial skepticism with a sensational round of batting practice, then leads his woebegone mates to a pennant reminiscent of Boston's 1914 Miracle Braves.

Second, Joe Hardy's relationship to the team and its management parallels that of Roy Hobbs in *The Natural*, including its use of the Arthurian motif. Roy joins the New York Knights and tries to relieve the suffering of manager and co-owner Pop Fisher (the Fisher King). Joe does the same for Pop's Washington counterpart, Benny van Buren, also a former third baseman, with "the eyes of a man who has known great suffering" (39). Not only a messiah, Joe is also cast as a knight and crusader come to slay the marauding monsters. In a dream "he saw a monster with a bloated, insatiable face, across its swollen chest the word YANKEES. He was striking the face with a baseball bat" (27). There are subsequent references to the "peerless monsters" (79) who "must have appeared seven feet tall to the opposing team" (83) and to a rival knight, the Yankee catcher, "like a giant in armor, standing there, blocking the plate" (232).

Pop Fisher's scheming partner, Judge Goodwill Banner, stands to benefit if the team does *not* win the pennant, and to that end the judge visits the ailing Roy Hobbs with a cash bribe not to play and win. Judge Banner can only operate in darkness and keeps the blinds drawn in his office with the lights dimmed. In Wallop's book, it is Applegate who corresponds to Banner, conspiring to make the hero's team lose and in the process shunning the light. "'Do you mind if I turn out the lights?' Applegate asked. 'When I'm conducting official business I don't like a great deal of light'" (53). The Senators' owner, Adam Welch, who has but months to live, is quite the opposite of Judge Banner. Visiting his bedridden star, Mr. Welch, thirsting though he is to win, considers it a clubowner's first duty to care for his players. "There's nothing so important as a man's health," he states, "not even winning a ball game" (159), and his trust is repaid at the end by Joe's heroics.

Third, in both novels the hero faces a nemesis at the ballpark. Joe Hardy's antagonist is a clown named Roscoe Ent, hired to pitch only as a diversion from the inept team.[1] Like Malamud's Bump Baily, who is benched in favor of Roy Hobbs, Ent despises Joe when he is dropped from the roster as the Hardy-led Senators make a run for the pennant, and he eventually conspires with Applegate in the deceitful eligibility hearing. Roscoe, standing barely five feet tall, also calls to mind Otto Zipp, the shrill, diminutive heckler of Roy Hobbs. At one point, Roy aims several batted balls at Zipp (in the film, he slugs them at Max Mercy, the Robert Duvall character). Joe Hardy considers the same thing against Applegate: "*Even if I can't hit the one we need,* he thought, *it would be the greatest pleasure in the world to hit a hard one foul into the right-field boxes, maybe catch Applegate off guard*" (231; Wallop's italics). Coincidentally, on the next pitch, "The ball *zipped* in" (231; my italics).

In a fourth parallel, both Joe Hardy and Roy Hobbs are dogged by a persistent reporter who seeks to prove them frauds. In *The Natural*, Max Mercy finally produces a photo that reveals Roy's shooting by Harriet Bird, while Luster Head, operating on an anonymous tip from Applegate, travels to Hannibal, Missouri, to check Joe's story about his hometown, prompting the commissioner to convene the hearing that could cost Joe his freedom. Applegate uses photos too—of the *future*—to show Joe what his life will be like with Lola and the Yankees. This proves to be the Devil's undoing, for

---

[1] In 1951, St. Louis Browns owner Bill Veeck signed a midget named Eddie Gaedel to pinch hit in a game against Cleveland. Gaedel walked, as expected, but American League President Will Harridge subsequently voided his contract and banned midgets from any further games.

when Joe sees himself in the Yankees photo, he is alerted to Applegate's plan and determines to foil it.

Fifth, each hero is caught between two women, and the resolution of the novels differs because of their reactions to the women. Roy Hobbs is enticed by the vamp Memo Paris to take money to throw the playoff game, rejecting (until it is too late) the sensible nurture of Iris Lemon, pregnant with his child. Joe Hardy refuses to abandon his team, but that loyalty almost costs him a return to his wife. Joe remains faithful to Bess but still allows the deadline to pass when he could return to her. At first, Lola resembles Memo, but later only her sacrificial love makes possible Joe's second chance. Indeed, Wallop may have grafted her and her name from Malamud's reference to Memo "looking like Lola, the Jersey City fortuneteller" (201).

Sixth, these two novels are similar in the colorful use of names. We have mentioned a few with mythological or religious connotations in *The Natural*: Pop the Fisher King; Roy the failed Grail King; Max(imum) Mercy, who doesn't show any; Judge Goodwill Banner, who also shows none and tries to throw the pennant (i.e., banner); plus coach Red Blow, the dwarf Otto Zipp, and the spiritually arid gambler Gus Sands. Consider too these ironic and playful monikers from *The Year the Yankees Lost the Pennant*: Joe Boyd, the Average Joe and Job, the patient, faithful, longsuffering Senators fan; Joe Hardy, so named because it "sounded rather athletic" (36), says Applegate; Applegate, suggesting the apple of the Fall and the gates of hell; owner Adam Welch, living under the curse of the Yankees, about to be redeemed; Yankee journalist Luster Head, whose head is *not* sacred or lustrous; Pitcher Sammy Ransom, who tries to "ransom" the lost/losers in the final game before Joe ultimately redeems them.

As with so many similar motifs in literary comparisons, it is rarely possible to say for sure that there is direct copying or inspiration, but taken together these motifs point convincingly to the conclusion that *The Natural*, written two years earlier, and not just *Faust* and the Bible, was prominent in Wallop's mind as he composed *The Year the Yankees Lost the Pennant*. The book did not arise in a vacuum, nor do I believe its light-hearted fantasy and religious imagery is necessarily without descendents in the development of baseball fiction. Though absolute links are not present, it is not unlikely that seeds from Joe Boyd's prophetic "call," being "chosen," his heeding a "voice," and pursuing a "dream," and from Joe Hardy's defeat of the aging process, his messianic sacrifice, and his faithful return back to the future took root in the fertile minds of W. P. Kinsella, Eric Rolfe Greenberg, and Darryl Brock. They would, I suspect, agree with Mike Shannon that *The Year the Yankees Lost the Pennant* is "one of the most underrated of the great works of baseball literature" (417).

Inning 2:

"Now Pitching...Joan of Arc":
Spitballs and Holy Water as a Missing Link

A little-known forerunner of great modern baseball fiction is James F. Donohue's 1977 novel *Spitballs and Holy Water*, which chronologically, stylistically, and thematically anticipates much of the magical realism of Jerome Charyn, W. P. Kinsella, Nancy Willard, and Darryl Brock, their reworking of modern American history, and their fascination with the religious qualities of baseball. I say "little known" not only because the novel was new to me when I purchased it sight unseen from a used book catalogue, but also because, save for the briefest notices in Andy McCue's bibliography of baseball books and a few publishers trade journals, I know of no serious mention of the book. Thus, it was with no little excitement that I contemplated the possibility of having stumbled onto something of a missing link between the landmark books it clearly echoes—Bernard

Malamud's *The Natural* (1952) and Robert Peterson's seminal study of Negro League baseball, *Only the Ball Was White* (1970)—and the delightful fiction that follows, which, I believe, it anticipates and probably even inspires. The novel may be "little known" to most readers, but, as I told one conference audience, I would bet my plane ticket home that Bill Kinsella knows it *very* well.

The narrator of this novel, writing in 1976, is a former Negro League star who documents a fantastic episode in the life of a latter-day Joan of Arc, a black Roman Catholic nun named Sister Timothy Stokes. At the behest of "voices" (of two saints, Margaret and Catherine) that she alone hears, Sister Timothy organizes a fantastic series between the Chicago American Giants, 1927 Negro League champions, and the legendary Murderers Row New York Yankees of Ruth, Gehrig, and Lazzeri, fresh from their 1927 World Series sweep of Pittsburgh. The financing for the series, also ordained by God and prompted by the voices, is an elaborate wager between a bizarre trinity of sponsors: the racist Ku Klux Klan, (giving 10-1 odds that the Yankees will prevail), the notorious gangster Al Capone (whose enormous wealth guarantees the wager), and the Catholic Church, which stands to win one million dollars if the underdog Giants, with Sister Timothy as pitcher(!), can defeat the mighty Yankees. It is God's will, she believes, that the million dollars be won to support the work of the church.

Against all odds, Sister Timothy not only brings the series to pass, but she also wins the first three games before huge crowds at Yankee Stadium. The key to uniting the disparate groups and to her phenomenal pitching ability is the nun's God-given power to stop time and manipulate events. However, like Joan of Arc, Sister Timothy runs afoul of power politics in both government and the church. New York governor Al Smith, seeking to be the nation's first Catholic president, fears that the series has "turned the

Roman Catholic Church into a monstrous band of slick operators about to win one million dollars and the Ku Klux Klan into a sympathetic choir of angels" (189). Smith wants her to stop the series, as does the church, which strongly supports the governor. The church worries that the series will severely harm his candidacy, and it prevails upon the Yankees to cancel the rest of the games. Moreover, the church tries the nun for witchcraft and convicts her of conspiracy with Satan.

In a nocturnal epilogue at an empty Yankee Stadium, Sister Timothy engages Satan in a bet reminiscent of Joe Hardy's encounter with Applegate in *The Year the Yankees Lost the Pennant* and roughly presaging Ben Harkissian's challenge to Death in *Things Invisible to See:* she wagers her soul that she can strike out Satan, and she does.

Spitballs and Holy Water is an entertaining fantasy of time-warp baseball, but it also has a serious underlay of urgent theological and social issues that define tensions in twentieth century America: segregation and race relations, prohibition and organized crime, politics and religion. The book, which appeared only in paperback, won a bronze medal from the *West Coast Review of Books* for fiction based on historical fact, and my discussion of the novel, beginning with a look at the main characters, will refer to that blend of fact and fiction. At the same time, I will comment on the author's literary and historical sources[1]—no novel in our study so clearly reveals its antecedents—and his potential influence on subsequent baseball fiction, especially that of W. P. Kinsella.

---

[1] The information about James F. Donohue's sources stems from an extensive phone interview with the author. I am extremely grateful to him for his kindness in sharing so much of the creative process involved in writing his novel.

Composite Characters

The book's narrator identifies himself as Robert Henry Lloyd, a former Negro League great, barnstormer, and most recently, school janitor, whose response to a question is the engaging opening of the novel: "Let's see now, you asked about Sister Timothy, the nun who struck out Babe Ruth. Well, I can tell you it was a wondrous occurrence" (5). Lloyd is writing in his old age, two years after the nun's death, drawing upon his memories of her baseball career, his continued correspondence with her, and her diary. The narrator himself is a composite character, fashioned primarily after John Henry "Pop" Lloyd (1884-1965), whom many consider the greatest short-stop of all time. Donohue has given him a different first name and different chronology (the narrator is writing in 1976, eleven years after Pop's pass-ing), but retains Lloyd's Cuban nickname—El Cuchara, the shovel—as recorded by Peterson in *Only the Ball Was White*. Where Pop Lloyd was nicknamed the "Black Wagner," Donohue's Lloyd is called the "Black Babe Ruth."[2] Some of Peterson's account of Satchel Paige's youth is also incor-porated into Lloyd's composite character, especially the five-year stay in an Alabama reform school, which provided education, insulation from bad influences, and a chance to play baseball.

Shovel Lloyd first encounters Sister Timothy at a barnstorming exhibi-tion near Boston when she strikes him out on three pitches, then does the same to his teammates and, later, to Babe Ruth. Lloyd is a reluctant but eventually faithful recruit who believes in Sister Timothy and her voices. Just as God has "chosen" the nun to arrange the series, so he has "called"

---

[2] Compare Peterson's quote of Honus Wagner, "I am honored to have John Lloyd called the Black Wagner. It is a privilege to have been compared with him" (74)—with Donohue's remark attributed to Babe Ruth, "I am honored to have Robert Henry Lloyd called the Black Babe Ruth. It is a privilege to have been compared with him" (26).

Shovel, she insists, and Lloyd agrees with wonder, adding: "I don't know why that nun picked me.... She had picked me, after all, picked a sinner" (70). He becomes her trusted assistant in arranging the series, her catcher and tutor during the games, and her "rudder" (79) in circumstances not clearly provided for by her voices.

The concept of being "chosen" is also prominent in Kinsella's work. In *Shoeless Joe*, published five years after *Spitballs*, the athletes who make the Major Leagues are "chosen"; so too are the spectators who believe sufficiently in the divine nature of the game that their eyes are opened to its beauty. J. D. Salinger is chosen by the ghostly players to enter their realm beyond the cornfield, and, of course, Ray Kinsella is chosen to build the cornfield ballpark. In the *Iowa Baseball Confederacy*, Matthew and Gideon Clarke refer to themselves as "chosen" and "prophets."[3]

Sister Timothy, like Shovel Lloyd, is also something of a composite character, but she is still *the* distinctive figure in the book, an American original in her own right. Interestingly, she has her genesis not in the most obvious parallel, Joan of Arc, but in the figure of Mattie Ross, the fourteen-year-old heroine of Charles Portis's 1968 novel, *True Grit*. Donohue was attracted to the "shrewd, self-confident ingenue" who convinces the crusty US marshal Rooster Cogburn (John Wayne's memorable film character) to enter Indian Territory to track down her father's killer. The author put Mattie's character into the 1920s, where she badgers another big lug, Babe Ruth, into carrying out her plan and prevails upon (i.e., blackmails) other authority figures to do her bidding. Donohue made the nun black to facilitate the connection to Negro League baseball, which lets her doubly tweak

---

[3] In *Havana Heat*, many years later, we also find Dummy Taylor called to a specific mission in Cuba—in a witch doctor's prophecy, by a Catholic priest's concern for a young boy, and in a priestess's ceremony.

the Klan, as both a black *and* a Catholic. Donohue's awareness of Peterson's book and interest in the Negro Leagues was initially stimulated by a SPORT magazine cover story commemorating Frank Robinson as the majors' first black manager in 1975. That article also featured other prominent black baseball figures, such as Rube Foster, owner and manager of the Chicago American Giants.

Only then did the Joan of Arc parallel emerge, a story that had fascinated Donohue as a Catholic youth. That theme was complemented by the 1950 bestseller (and later film) *The Cardinal,* by Henry Morton Robinson, in which Father Stephen Fermoyle's conflicts with the church suggested another dimension to Donohue. Indeed, the church villains in *Spitballs and Holy Water* are two cardinals, one who is skimming money from church coffers, and another who tries Sister Timothy for witchcraft.

The religious plot is intertwined with the baseball plot, each with its own set of pressing questions. The baseball questions are, first, will the series ever come off? That is, can the nun possibly make allies, or at least business partners, out of such different and antagonistic groups: the Southern Klan and New York *Yankees,* for heaven's sake; the Klan and blacks; the Klan and Catholics; Protestants and Catholics; the church and organized crime; white baseball and black baseball? And second, once the series is arranged, who will win? Will the nun's powers carry the day, or will they desert her on Murderers Row?

The religious questions are, first, does Sister Timothy *really* hear voices, and are they and her powers divine or demonic?[4] (The narrator, Shovel Lloyd, admits with great shame that he too wondered "if the Black Devil

---

[4] Similar questions are raised in *Things Invisible to See* and *Havana Heat.* Who, we wonder, is creating the prophecies and working the miracles, and by what power?

might not be more with her than the Lord" [75], but he is later convinced of their divine nature.) The second great religious question is, what will be Sister Timothy's fate in the church? Will she fare any better than did Joan of Arc? These issues combine to produce a creative tension throughout the novel and take it beyond mere humorous fantasy.

Messing with Time, and Other Themes

If Sister Timothy is the distinctive character in *Spitballs and Holy Water*, her ability to stop time is the brainstorm that kick-starts the novel. The idea came to Donohue, he says, as he recalled childhood fantasies of starring in baseball and football games by being able to manipulate time. He gives this ability to Sister Timothy—she uses it in baseball by moving the ball behind the bat while all around her are frozen—without which the nun would neither have arranged the series nor starred in it.

The nun's manipulation of time is a delightful device and one that points ahead to Kinsella (also to Charyn and Willard), much of whose work has a "Back to the Future" quality. *Shoeless Joe* and *The Iowa Baseball Confederacy*, for instance, are based on the premise that time is malleable, though Kinsella generally has his characters move back and forth through "cracks in time" more than stopping it to manipulate events.[5]

---

[5] The star player of Charyn's barnstorming team in *The Seventh Babe* was "Pharaoh the enchanter, who could step out of the ordinary workings of time, and appear to float while he was making the most savage and impossible leap" (157). In the séance of *Things Invisible to See*, participants "felt as if they were in another corner of the universe, dabbling and dipping themselves in the streams of no-time" (112). Later, "time stopped on the high seas" (192), and Death admits to "a little finagling with current events" (195).

Other literary motifs in *Spitballs* show Donahue's reliance on Malamud and his role as something of a bridge to Kinsella, for example in depicting the baseball as a white pigeon or dove.

> *The Natural*—At thirty-three the Whammer still enjoyed exceptional eyesight. He saw the ball spin off Roy's fingertips and it reminded him of a white pigeon he had kept as a boy, that he would send into flight by flipping it into the air. The ball flew at him and he was conscious of its bird-form and white flapping wings, until it suddenly disappeared from view (28).

> *Spitballs*—At thirty-eight, I still had the eyesight of an eagle. I saw the ball spin off the nun's fingertips, and it reminded me of a white pigeon I had kept as a boy, which I would send into flight by flipping it into the air. The ball flew at me, and I watched its bird-form and white flapping wings, coming, coming, so everloving slow (10-11).

> *The IBC*—The ball soars as if it has a life of its own, as if it has grown feathers, and like a white dove it flies toward infinity (286).

Donohue's passage parallels Malamud's in another respect: it comes during the confrontation of an aging star with an unknown phenom. Just as young Roy Hobbs fans the Whammer at the train stop, so the frail Sister Timothy commands sudden respect by striking out Shovel Lloyd and then the Babe at the American Legion field in Chelsea, Massachusetts.

In this confrontation, like Malamud and Kinsella elsewhere, Donohue uses the presence of lightning to denote a momentous event on the ball field and a suggestion of God's (or gods') agency. Sister Timothy does not view her ability to stop time as a gimmick, but as a gift to be used with great devotion. When Babe Ruth "walked like a god to the batter's box" (31) to face the nun, the moment seemed "consecrated" (33). "The world, stilled that way, was like deep prayer for her. Ecstasy of the soul. She told me this must be what it was like for the saints when they were caught up in the rapture of God" (34). When Ruth struck out, "the sky turned suddenly black and a flash of jagged lightning cut the clouds" (36). The climax of this showdown echoes Good Friday, when Christ's death prompted darkening of the sun and the rending of the temple veil.[6]

Two other borrowings by Donohue from Malamud are the dwarf heckler, Otto P. Zipp, and the assault with a line drive foul ball. Here is how the two authors describe them:

> *The Natural*—The dwarf honked a loud horn at the end of a two-foot walking stick, and it sounded as if a flock of geese had been let loose at the offenders, driving them—his purple curses ringing in their ears—to seek shelter in some hidden hole in the stands or altogether out of the ballpark (76-77).

> *Spitballs*—The dwarf wore a brown suit and carried a megaphone in one hand and a horn at the end of a two-foot walking stick in the other. By squeezing the horn's rubber bulb, he got a sound like a flock of geese let loose (30).

Because his figure was so clearly taken from Malamud, Donohue wondered if he shouldn't call him Zipp. His editor advised him to create another name, and so came the elaborate handle, Thurmond Z. [for Zipp?] Feeney.

---

[6] Lightning strikes near Dummy Taylor in *Havana Heat*, punctuating his encounter with *santería*, just before he "felt myself slip over the edge of somewhere I'd never been" (296).

Though the characters are obviously cut from the same cloth, there is an intriguing difference that shows another literary bridge between Malamud, Donohue, and Kinsella. Consider the first two:

> *The Natural*—On the next pitch he shortened his hold on Wonderboy, stepped in front of the ball, and pulled it sharply foul.... Roy tried to send the next ball through his teeth.... Roy chopped a third foul at the dwarf. With a shriek he covered his face with his arms and ducked.... At the last split second he had tried to hold his swing but couldn't. The ball spun like a shot at Otto, struck his hard skull with a thud, and was deflected upward (223).

> *Spitballs*—The Babe hit her next pitch on a line drive right to the middle of Feeney's forehead. It dropped the midget like a shot. Unblinking and unmoving, Feeney watched the ball coming at him. Even from where I squatted behind the plate I could make out the look of surprise and horror on the ugly little face. The oncoming ball must have hypnotized him (143).

Malamud's passage portrays the dwarf as a scrambling target in a shooting gallery,[7] while Donohue has him freezing before a single drive, focusing on the ball. Kinsella adopts the line drive incident in *The Iowa Baseball Confederacy*, where the narrator's father perishes at the ball park:

> *The IBC*—Bill Bruton, the Milwaukee center fielder, swung late at a Harvey Haddix fast ball and sent it screaming over the top of the

---

[7] In the film of *The Natural*, Robert Redford as Roy Hobbs bats balls at the sports writer, Max Mercy, played by Robert Duvall. There is no Zipp character, and the incident takes place in an empty ballpark.

visitors' dugout, at a speed of more than a hundred miles per hour. My father was writing on his scorecard and supposedly never saw the ball, which struck him full on the left temple, bursting a blood vessel and killing him instantly (49).

But Kinsella then modifies the scene brilliantly by revealing that Matthew Clarke was not struck accidentally as was first suspected. Gideon had seen the ball's reflection in his father's eye and knew that Matthew had actually committed suicide by focusing carefully on the line drive, then leaning slightly into the ball to absorb the fatal blow.

A final comparison between Donohue and Kinsella returns us to the use of religion in their baseball novels. Kinsella, as we shall see, delightfully portrays the religious qualities of the game of baseball and teases baseball fans who love their game with a religious fervor. He jokes about "the great god Baseball" and the "chosen ones" who spread the "baseball gospel."[8] Ray Kinsella, like Joan of Arc and Sister Timothy, hears and heeds a voice that establishes his mission. *Shoeless Joe* even includes the travesty of a religious revival—"That is the living word of baseball.... Praise the name of baseball. The word will set captives free" (193). Both that novel and *The Iowa Baseball Confederacy* express severe disapproval of fundamental Christianity, which Kinsella, a card-carrying atheist, sees as joyless and intolerant.

Donohue, a practicing Roman Catholic, does criticize the shortcomings of his church, especially in the villainous cardinals, but generally with humor, and he clearly admires the devotion as well as the spunk of Sister

---

[8] *Things Invisible to See* doesn't so much proclaim the gospel of baseball as it attributes a divine origin to the game. Its sensational opening sentence reads, "In Paradise, on the banks of the River of Time, the Lord of the Universe is playing ball with His archangels" (3).

Timothy. He chronicles the hostility of (especially Southern) Protestantism to Catholicism, but recognizes the genuine Baptist faith, the salvation, and the contented life of Shovel Lloyd. Though some question Sister Timothy's sanity (as the Iowans later do with Ray Kinsella), Shovel, we know, believes in the nun's divine call. The reader, however, is not sure until the final scene. After all, if the nun is doing God's will, why would he abandon her to politics and sabotage the series?

This is what Sister Timothy wonders in the novel's final scene at Yankee Stadium. "What is it I was supposed to accomplish?" she angrily asks God. (Ray Kinsella wonders the same thing, and each time he thinks he has the answer—build the park, ease Salinger's pain, let Doc Graham play in the majors—he is called to yet another purpose: to reconcile with his father.) The answer for Sister Timothy comes when she extracts a promise from the Devil that, should she strike him out, fifty years hence a black man would break Babe Ruth's home run record and do it in the heart of Klan country, Atlanta. Because Satan can also move in and out of time, Sister Timothy's special power is negated. She must resort to another device to whiff the Devil and win her bet: a spitball, soaked in holy water. "'You tricked me!,' screamed Satan. 'Oh, go to hell,' Sister Timothy said, and inside her wrinkled skin her little-girl soul did handsprings" (204).

The little-girl soul, Mattie Ross, Joan of Arc, was not lost, nor was it burned at the stake. Instead, the divine purpose was accomplished, not of winning a million dollars, but of preparing the way for justice and healing in American society. In constructing a fanciful story that draws on American history, religious culture, and baseball fiction, James F. Donohue has created a significant if heretofore missing link to the artistic imagination of W. P. Kinsella and other great baseball novelists.

Identity Crisis and Folk Religion in *The Seventh Babe*

Overview

Jerome Charyn's *The Seventh Babe* is the first novel in our series that focuses more on folk religion than on a traditional faith. Like its two closest descendants, *Things Invisible to See* and *Havana Heat*, it has a whirl of powerful, sometimes disturbing images blended with fantastic action that stretches the reader's credulity. Because it also has an extremely complex plot not widely known to the reading public, we will summarize it briefly before considering in some detail the two main issues of this chapter: Charyn's desperate portrayal of human identity, and man's use of American voodoo in an attempt to find himself in baseball.

The 1979 novel consists of 23 chapters in 9 books totaling 345 pages. The first four books take us only from 1923 to 1925; the last five race

through time to 1978. They chronicle the adult life and bizarre baseball career of one Babe Ragland, or Rags (the nom de glove of Cedric Tannehill, son of a copper and beef magnate), a left-handed third baseman who makes the 1923 Boston Red Sox team as an unknown seventeen-year-old. On-field adjustments to hazing by resentful veterans are complicated by his off-field relationship to the seductive, red-haired mother-daughter tandem of Marylou and Iva Cottonmouth. These "witches" are respectively close friend and ward of Sox owner and theatrical producer Hollis McKee, alias Harry Frazee, the man who sold Babe Ruth to the Yankees in 1920 and inflicted on Boston the "Curse of the Bambino."

After two successful seasons, Babe marries Iva, heiress to an ice fortune, but the marriage soon sours. When in 1925 (book 5) he is framed by McKee and banned from major league baseball, Rags and his former roommate, the hunchbacked team mascot Scarborough,[1] join the Cincinnati Colored Giants, a traveling Negro team on which he is the only white player. Here Rags is introduced to the voodoo of the team's witch doctor, who endues the entire entourage with magical powers that let them excel on the field and survive in the hostile, racist society of the 1920s South. In the 1930s (book 6), the witch doctor leaves the Giants and the team owner drifts into insanity,[2] so Rags buys the club and becomes its magician. Baseball commissioner Judge Landis learns of McKee's frame-up and offers to reinstate Rags, who, except for a brief later appearance with the St. Louis Browns, prefers to stay with his club and with Iva, with whom he has reconciled.

---

[1] Major league teams often had official, adult mascots, such as the short-statured Eddie Bennett, who doubled as batboy for the New York Yankees from 1921 to 1933. Charyn's Scarborough follows similar characters in *The Natural*, *The Year the Yankees Lost the Pennant*, and *Spitballs and Holy Water*, and prefigures Little Walter, the Cubs' hunchbacked midget mascot in *The Iowa Baseball Confederacy*.

[2] This is perhaps a take-off on the sad fate of Negro League legend Rube Foster (1879-1930), who also played a prominent role in *Spitballs and Holy Water*.

The last twenty-nine years of the story are telescoped into two bizarre episodes in books 8 and 9—an encounter with the dead Scarborough, who now haunts a forest as a demon, and the kidnapping/liberation of his old teammate, Garland James, from a Massachusetts nursing home. Heeding voices that tell him to "Go with the Giants," the seventy-nine-year-old James joins the seventy-four-year-old Babe to barnstorm through time.[3]

Magical Realism

Although much in Charyn's novel echoes *The Natural* and *Spitballs and Holy Water*, its primary inspiration has to be the works of the Colombian writer Gabriel García Márquez, especially *One Hundred Years of Solitude* (1967).[4] Of García Márquez it is written that his basic themes are "violence, solitude, and the overwhelming need for love" (*Columbia Encyclopedia*, 1043), and much the same could be said of Charyn in *The Seventh Babe*. The stylistic means both men use to develop these themes are generally referred to as "magical realism": a realistic description of life, often in minute detail, that merges naturally with the account of "antirational,"[5] highly improbable, or physically impossible happenings. Realistic and mag-

---

[3] This scene may owe a debt to the Chief's escape in *One Flew Over the Cuckoo's Nest* (1962) and foreshadows several related baseball capers: Salinger's kidnapping and later rapture in *Shoeless Joe*; Ben Harkissian's bolting from the hospital to play the showdown ballgame against Death in *Things Invisible to See*; and the liberation of Irwin in *The Brothers K*. It also anticipates the 1989 film *The Dream Team*, in which mental patients are taken to Yankee Stadium.

[4] In an interview with Frederic Tuten, Charyn admits to only three influences: Ernest Hemingway (especially *The Sun Also Rises*), William Faulkner's *The Sound and the Fury*, and García Márquez's *One Hundred Years of Solitude*. He later adds Herman Melville, Vladimir Nabokov, and William James as others he admires. García Márquez also cites Faulkner as a primary influence in his own work.

[5] Cf. Raymond L. Williams's summary of García Márquez's art: his "redefinition of realism implies a faithfulness to a higher truth, a mythical level of reality that a more pedestrian realism cannot comprehend. These three factors—antirationality, transcendent regionalism, and myth—are integral to the aesthetics and universality of García Márquez's fiction" (615).

ical events follow one upon another, often outside of time, and the reader is flooded with images and associations that create a rich, literary jambalaya but also disorder and disorientation. The authors' fascination with these images and themes is striking—many of them appear ten, twenty, thirty, or more times. Charyn's favorites, several of which overlap with García Márquez, are ice,[6] copper, blood, swamps, snakes, tongues, dreams, time (and timelessness), madness, evil and the Devil, lust (vs. love), voodoo, death, and ghosts. We will look at some of these themes in the following pages, but it is not necessary to analyze each of them to understand their cumulative effect on the reader, who is bombarded by colorful, disconnected, often grotesque literary associations. The sheer volume of them is a key to the style of magical realism.

Human Identity

The Seventh Babe is a good example of a baseball novel that is more a statement about life than a sports story. Charyn uses baseball here to create a slice of American cultural history and a highly charged, rough-edged vision of human existence. The ups and downs of Babe Ragland's baseball career are subordinated to the overriding issue of man's fate in a turbulent world, specifically the questions of human identity posed in the novel: "Who was he? Cedric Tannehill, or the seventh Babe? ...Would someone tell the kid who he was?" (111, 168).

One answer to these questions of identity lies in Charyn's desperate image of man and the world. Despite the never-say-die gameness of Babe

---

[6] Ice is mentioned in the famous first sentence of *One Hundred Years of Solitude* and reappears several times in the novel. In *The Seventh Babe*, it is the source of wealth for Iva, whose father is an ice-producing magnate.

Ragland, the world in which he casts about for relief or escape is depicted as a primordial swamp, a haunted forest, a cold, menacing society, a grave-yard. "'What kind of frigging world is this, where cops can become babysitters in a Boston speakeasy?' 'The same frigging world that stole Babe Ruth from us and turned the Sox into a cemetery'" (78). And rural fans watching local teams lose to the barnstormers and their witch doctor "returned to their villages resigned to the reality of an evil world, where black devils couldn't lose" (155).

In this evil world, man is portrayed as an animal, insecure,[7] lacking a true identity, and failing in the search for lasting human intimacy. In suggesting man's animal nature, Charyn does not so much directly label his characters as particular animals or portray them as predator and prey. Rather, he gives them animal attributes—claws, for example, instead of hands, and snakes for coils of hair[8]—and generously employs common expressions that keep animal imagery in the reader's mind. In small doses or in a kinder context, this would not be so significant, for when someone is called "a monkey," it might mean little more than "rascal." To "monkey" with something can mean merely "fiddle" or "fool around." Cumulatively, however, even when used in a standard way, the expressions assail the human image through incessant association with animals. For example, Rags crouches on the field "like a monkey" (29) and does a "monkey dance" (33); going out at night he wears fancy "monkey clothes" (83). Racist fans refer to black players as "monkeys" and "baboons" (155), and inept white players "look like complete monkeys" (158). The same holds true for other

---

[7] Charyn's own insecurity is a good example. He says, "I feel incompetent, childlike, in every way outside of the writing…to me, the world seems so perversely magical that I never believe anything is going to turn out right. I'm always terrorized" (Tuten 102-103).

[8] Serpents play a large role in later baseball novels, especially *The Iowa Baseball Confederacy* and *Havana Heat*.

examples: dogs, frogs, crows, lizards,[9] which though used in a standard literal or figurative sense, as a noun or a verb, only reinforce the negative image attributed to human beings. We are told that "The kid developed a dinosaur's eye for open spaces. And a coyote's ear.... Rags defined himself against the territory of an infield and the smack of horsehide on wood like a prairie animal" (145-46).

Other non-human appellations tarnish the human image, such as "spook," "phantom," "ghost," "demon," and "devil." These words, which are used figuratively throughout the novel (but also literally to describe the magical appearance of the dead), suggest Babe Ragland's flight from his past, his exile at the hands of Judge Landis, and the marginalized social position of the blacks—the invisible men, in Ralph Ellison's term[10]—and the difficulty of all people to be secure in an identity.

Another aspect of the identity issue is that human nature itself is in flux, implying not only an adaptability and elusiveness, but also uncertainty and insecurity. Marylou and her daughter Iva are interchangeable, both in appearance and in their relationship to the men they seduce. Scarborough, "the brute" as he is often called, is alternately a lumberjack, batboy/mascot, roommate/teammate, friend/betrayer, and, in death, "monster of Sackville Forest" (331). The "phantoms" of the Cincinnati Colored Giants are not really from Cincinnati and can't even find their identity in playing ball. They must be clowns to survive, adapting themselves to each situation, imitating the style and mannerisms of white ballplayers.[11]

---

[9] Looking ahead to *Things Invisible to See*, we read of the root doctor "Cold Friday withering into a lizard, which warmed its thin claws over the fire and sang" (247).

[10] Indeed, Charyn writes, "The majors were buying up colored ballplayers, and then these ballplayers turned invisible" (325).

Above all, it is Babe Ragland who has so many identities that he has none: "The kid had too many selves in that house. Ragland, Cedric, Harvard Jack. Everybody and nobody all at once" (168). We learn that his mother died when he was but six, and his father was distant. The vicious treatment (and subsequent death) of his servant boy by the father's handymen was an indelible memory of his youth and a key reason why he rejected his privileged upbringing and assumed a new identity based on the Babe Ruth legend: a left-handed orphan from Baltimore who asserts himself in baseball. The kid was at once drawn to the perceived idyll of baseball and fleeing the horror of death and cruelty he knew at home. He soon finds that baseball has its own cruelty and death, but the pattern of adaptation continues. Richard Gaughran calls Babe's identity quest "a cyclical pattern of role-playing.... He assumes a role, facts from the outside intrude, so he alters his role or adopts a new one. This new role is then challenged, and the pattern continues" (93). Rags is, as Gaughran points out, in turn Cedric Tannehill, the beloved seventh Babe, "the bad boy of baseball" (190), "Bossman" of the Giants (273), "magician Rags" (276), and "entrepreneur of a wandering baseball club" (281). In game promotions, "He was advertised as 'Mr. Babe Ragland, Refugee of the White American League, The Boy Who Was Driven out of Baseball by Kenesaw Mountain Landis, And Is Now a Fixture at Third Base for the Cincinnati Giants'" (225). Ultimately, writes Gaughran, "Ragland finds life in his role as an outlaw" (94).

Another answer to Babe's identity question is that of a married man. Babe's marriage to the teenaged Iva, as indeed every other male-female relationship in the novel, is marked by misunderstanding, infidelity, and

---

[11] See the article by Richard Gaughran, who has much to say about the "protean tendencies" of Rags and his associates, especially Scarborough.

frustration; it does not let him find his identity in a lasting relationship with another person.[12] Once again his situation is representative of mankind, which finds human intimacy an illusion. Again recalling García Márquez, we find the human need for love answered by solitude.

Rags learns early on in his career that "There's no such thing as a married man on the Red Sox…. The Sox were without one legitimate baseball wife" (14, 22), and he himself has no desire to marry. Even when engaged, "He was more of a bachelor now than somebody's fiancée" (94). The closest relationship in the book is that shared with his roommate, Scarborough. "A roomie was as sacred as a wife" (118) with whom he shares "a honeymoon" (122) of chocolate sodas. When the time comes to marry, Rags insists on bringing Scarborough along. "I have a roommate," he insists, "and I'm not going to desert him…. He'll die if he has to live alone" (123).

Babe vainly hopes that marriage will solve his identity dilemma: "*Cedric's dead. Cedric's dead. I'm Babe Ragland. I have a wife*" (140; Charyn's italics). Immediately, however, he learns of his (supposedly virgin) bride's violation by the family servant and regrets that he and Iva have moved in with her mother: "It was a dog's life. A bride who'd been punctured by another man; a mother-in-law who lay down with boys in the swamp because she loved Garland James and couldn't have him; a roommate who lived in a rat's hole two floors under Rags…. He was the most miserable husband on earth" (145-46).

Shortly after his marriage, Rags goes on the road, rejecting Iva's request to accompany him. The marriage quickly deteriorates when at Christmas

---

[12] Charyn's interview again reveals similarities to his own life. "I come from a family that I find very bizarre. I've been angry at my mother for a long, long time, and it's only recently that I've gotten rid of this anger. I was never really able to break out of my family and form my own family…. In some way, all my work involves family ties, family relationships" (Tuten 102).

Rags takes Iva into her mother's bed, and Iva takes revenge by sleeping with the entire team at spring training. Rags returns to the Boston hotel to live with Scarborough, and when, after Marylou's suicide, he tries to rejoin Iva, she won't take him back. Neither will the fans: "The golden days were finished.... He was the bad boy of baseball" (187).

Bad marriage also marks life with the Cincinnati Colored Giants, in the relationship between Emma and Carl Raines, the co-owners of the team. Emma takes other men, including Rags, and leaves the team at will to return to her native New Orleans. Her mercurial nature contributes to Carl's madness and frustrates Rags, who longs more for her than for any woman, until her murder by the pimp, Marshall Glove.

Heeding the voices that speak to him through his magical equipment, Babe returns to Iva, who at first agrees only to be his roommate in the Hudson automobile; eventually they live as man and wife: "It took twenty-six years" (321).

Religious Motifs

As noted above, *The Seventh Babe* is distinctive in its treatment of religion in that it is the first baseball novel to deal with voodoo and folk religion, not mainstream faith. Like *Spitballs and Holy Water*, it shows the sinister nature of spiritual warfare, but with no connection to Roman Catholicism and with many devils rather than *the* Devil of the Bible. The star black player, Pharaoh Yarbull, has the same power as Donohue's black nun or several of W. P. Kinsella's and Nancy Willard's characters to stop, or step outside of, time. Charyn's novel may well have suggested several themes or details to them (secret voices, ghostly ballplayers, magical and muddy games, magical snakes and roots), but Charyn has virtually no New

Testament perspective, whereas Kinsella does. The latter sharply criticizes Protestant fundamentalism in both *Shoeless Joe* and *The Iowa Baseball Confederacy*, but he also is positive in expressing the power of baseball and human imagination in Christian terms. The Iowa ball field suggests a heaven for the ballplayers, and the cornfield does the same for the "raptured" J. D. Salinger. The apocalyptic vision of *The IBC* appears to draw heavily on imagery of *The Seventh Babe* and other baseball novels.

The God of the Bible, capital G, is mentioned once in Charyn's novel, by the ghost of Marylou, while there are numerous references to the "gods of Fenway" (21), "rain gods" (236), "local gods" (343), and "baseball gods" (330). Judge Landis is called both a god and high priest (215), from whom the banished Rags refuses to ask "forgiveness" or "redemption." Interestingly, when Babe's innocence is established, it is the judge who seeks forgiveness and redemption from him. (Rather than a god, Judge Landis represents the Devil in *Shoeless Joe* for banning Joe Jackson.)

There are two prominent Old Testament allusions, even if neither is explicitly labeled: the primitive state of creation in Genesis and the magical duels in Exodus. Unlike in Genesis, the world in *The Seventh Babe* is not paradise, and there is no benevolent Creator who pronounces his handiwork "good." The basic condition of the world reminds one more of the primordial chaos when "the earth was without form and void" (Gen 1:2) than of the finished Eden. The setting is the Fens, the swamp near which Fenway Park was built, filled with heavy foliage, mud, and murky water. It is the scene of sexual seduction and license and finally of death, Marylou's suicide. Death, in fact, is a constant companion of man in this novel, claiming many characters and referred to dozens of times in the narration. At first glance, one might think of Fenway Park as a civilized Fens, an Eden, with its manicured field and ordered activity, and certainly Babe Ragland hopes it will be, but he soon learns that its refinements are only superficial. There are still snakes (Snake Attreau, the Cottonmouths), curses (by the mascot hunchbacks), hostility (fistfights among the players), and dark dampness (in the tunnels).

There are other indications that the world of the Red Sox is the fallen Eden of Genesis. Marylou, the seductress of the Fens, is associated with the serpent of the garden, first in her surname—Cottonmouth, a venomous swamp snake also called a water moccasin—and second in her gorgon-like hair that looks to Rags like "a bushel of snakes: red snakes about to uncoil" (60). The snake motif is most common in this book, used in names, as a verb, and in metaphors. Marylou's daughter is Iva, which can also be pronounced Eva, that is, Eve. Iva prefers her fine neighborhood to the swamp, but even its local park reminds one of the fall of man: "The park had a gate around it with different kinds of spears running along the top. Someone had stuck an apple into one of these spears; the apple bled a strange pink from its open wound" (45). Finally, Hollis McKee's musical about baseball wives is called *Eveline*, also a take-off on the name Eve, and McKee, as mentioned above, is the man who brought a curse to the paradise of Fenway Park, the "Curse of the Bambino."

The second half of the novel is dominated by voodoo, a practice that originated in West Africa and came to the US via the slave trade. Babe Ragland first encounters voodoo on a barnstorming tour against the Cincinnati Colored Giants. The Giants, it seems, have their own witch doctor, one Samuel Sharn, who blesses the entire entourage. Their superb skills alone make them a worthy opponent, but the presence of a medicine man makes them appear superhuman. The star of the Giants—and this is where the Exodus parallel begins—is named Pharaoh Yarbull. (This is another significant name: Pharaoh = ruler of ancient Egypt, Moses' antagonist; Yar =

agile + bull; hence, a strong and agile player.) "He was Pharaoh the enchanter, who could step out of the ordinary workings of time, and appear to float while he was making the most savage and impossible leap; the Pharaoh could trim down his moves and translate them into absolute energy. It came with a price. He forced his body beyond what other men could do. But that terrifying tension he induced in the field had aged him" (157). Only with the help of the witch doctor can he stave off the aging process and keep playing.

When Rags decides that the white all-stars can win only by countering the Giants with voodoo of their own, he enlists Scarborough to learn the witch doctor's craft. Thus begins a confrontation like that of Exodus 7-12, in which God through Aaron and Moses visits ten plagues on the Egyptians to demonstrate his sovereignty, humble Pharaoh, and set the Hebrews free. The Pharaoh's magicians match Aaron's feat of turning his rod into a serpent, and they duplicate the first two plagues, transforming the Nile into blood and covering the land with frogs. However, at the third one, the plague of gnats, the magicians fail and concede, "This is the finger of God" (8:19).

Challenged by Scarborough, Samuel is outraged and threatens the all-stars with "plague," "boils," and "frogs" (159), and indeed they are stricken by dysentery. But eventually Scarborough is able to negate Samuel's power. "Rags mustered whatever totems he could think of.... He reckoned that Scarborough's hump would behave like a lightning rod and drink up the Giants' voodoo" (162). Then the witch doctor brings out his magical root[13] (agent of his power, like Aaron's rod) and shakes it in its jar, causing rain and darkness to disrupt the game[14] and drive away the spectators. Strangely, however, the rain does not fall on the all-stars; it only slows up Yarbull's final bid for a home run, keeping it in the park for the final out. As in Exodus, the Pharaoh is defeated by a greater power. "Goodbye, Pharaoh" (165).

Except when Scarborough is present, the magician's root continues to be effective, letting Samuel predict the future, curse the living, raise the dead, and appease the rain gods. When Samuel finally leaves the club, Rags offers to become the team magician and work the root. But when it is unable to revive the dying Scarborough, Rags rejects the root, bringing another clear parallel to Exodus. "Disaster struck the Giants. Locusts ate the wood off a Buick. Diamonds would freeze up and split along the base lines. Storm clouds followed the team. Bullfrogs would leap out of the mud to plague the magician and his men.... All these visitations only served to harden Rags" (291). He hardens like the biblical Pharaoh but soon softens and takes "out the jar to save his team. ...Without his knowing it, Rags grew kinder to the root. Hairs sprouted on one of its three forks" (291); this is an echo of Aaron's rod blossoming in the book of Numbers (17:8). Then, with Yarbull having left the team, Rags, owner and magician, also becomes the star of the team, the new Pharaoh.

Folk religion serves two main purposes in *The Seventh Babe*. First, it is a splendid vehicle for Charyn's magical realism that blends local color and cultural history with fantastic events. Complementing the Old Testament imagery, voodoo brings the reader into a world populated by demons, ghosts, and strange magicians. The magic here is not as benign as in, for

---

[13] Magical roots and root imagery equated with snakes are prominent in *Things Invisible to See* and *The IBC*. While Charyn uses the term "rootworker," Willard calls her folk healer a "root doctor." "A hoodoo root doctor," writes Nicole McCleod, "must have the power to negotiate with spirits in order to deal with situations in the physical world. The root doctor's power can be used for good or evil, depending on the doctor and the issue at hand.... Root doctors are herbalists who use various plant and animal parts to cure or create ailments" (1).

[14] Cf. *The Iowa Baseball Confederacy*, where forty days of rain deluge the game.

example, *Shoeless Joe,* where a benevolent force envelops Kinsella's kindly dreamers, blesses their lives, and lets them slip through "a crack in time" to attain their heart's desire. Instead, Charyn's magic is a chaotic, disturbing force that is seized by his characters and wielded as a weapon of survival—on the ball field, in a hostile society, and in the struggle against time and death.

This ties into the second main function of voodoo, which is to let Babe Ragland pursue his dual obsessions, playing baseball and fleeing death and the consequences of aging. His flight is initially from the brutal world of his father and the responsibility that comes with being heir to the Tannehill fortune. Rags simultaneously embraces the world of the blacks, from whom he first learns baseball and whom he later joins on the barnstorming circuit. Baseball, a boy's game, lets him be Peter Pan. If he stays forever young, he resists death, and the power of voodoo lets him do that, even as he rescues Garland James from a living death in the nursing home to follow the magical voices and "*Go with the Giants, go with the Giants*" (345).

Inning 4:

The Great God Baseball: *Shoeless Joe,* Religious Magic, and the American Dream

As alluded to in the introduction, W. P. Kinsella's first novel, *Shoeless Joe,* was my gateway to adult baseball fiction, and getting to spend several hours speaking with Kinsella gave me an extra sense of kinship with his work. Since then I have shared it with church groups interested in the spiritual dimensions of the novel and film, with colleagues skeptical of anything having to do with baseball, and with my students, one of whom wrote me months later to thank me for introducing her to "The Magic of W. P. Kinsella." Thus it is a special pleasure to present it here to my readers, trusting that they will warm to its humor, fantasy, and gentle paean to the American dream.

Since I first wrote on W. P. Kinsella's *Shoeless Joe* in 1986, more articles have appeared on this book than on any other covered in this study, and

several address the question of religion. While there is understandably some common ground among us, each critic stresses different qualities of the novel. Brian Aitken, for instance, interprets *Shoeless Joe* according to Joseph Campbell's three phases of "monomyth": departure, initiation, and return. Rebecca Easton believes the book "can be read allegorically as the process by which a writer creates a piece of fiction" (121). Robert Hamblin focuses on Kinsella's literary form, his signature "magical realism" (which we discussed in chapter 3 on *The Seventh Babe*), and dubs the author "a literary 'pitcher'" who "commands a wide assortment of deliveries" (4) that blend fiction and reality. Richard Alan Schwartz sees in *Shoeless Joe* "a fairy tale structure" (137), while other critics see the book as an example of pastoralism. Nicholas J. Mount places the novel in "the idealistic school of pastoral" (65), and Bobby Fong sees at the heart of the book and its film version, *Field of Dreams*, "a pastoral vision compounded of yearning and faith" (31). That so many different readings of *Shoeless Joe* are possible testifies to the richness of the novel, its pivotal position in the history of baseball fiction, and its ability to engage a reader's imagination and fantasy.

Genuine Fantasy

A current fad of affluent America is the Sports Fantasy Camp. For the ungodly sum of something like $3,995, middle-aged baseball fans join the heroes of their youth in a one-week training camp. Members of the 1969 Cubs, 1963 Dodgers, or 1961 Yankees usher them into the never-never land of life on a major league club, tutor them in rusty (or never-were) baseball skills, and thump them back to reality in a climactic game between old heroes and eternally young hero-worshipers.

Now if the reader, too, would enjoy rolling back the clock, rubbing elbows with childhood baseball idols, and being privy to the sounds, smell, and feel of *real* baseball but doesn't have a spare $3,995 lying around, then W.P. Kinsella's fantasy baseball novel *Shoeless Joe* is just the thing—and in paperback it's $3,983 cheaper than the camps.

Kinsella's book is named for Shoeless Joe Jackson, the immensely talented outfielder of the Chicago White Sox, dubbed the "Black Sox," who was one of eight players banned from baseball for their role in dumping the 1919 World Series to underdog Cincinnati. Just as the fate of Jackson has caused many a fan to wonder "what might have been" had he been allowed to resume his career, so this novel explores the same question in the lives of the author, his family, and several fanciful acquaintances. At the same time, it illustrates the broad appeal of baseball for American culture and uses the sport as a vehicle for discussing such human endeavors as dreaming, magic, love, family, and religion.

Shoeless Joe defies easy description. It blends past and present, biography and invention, crisscrossing "that tingling line between fantasy and reality" (cited in Murray, 37). It reminds one of such typically American works as *Harvey, Our Town, The Wizard of Oz,* and, in the context of our study, *The Year the Yankees Lost the Pennant* and *Spitballs and Holy Water.*[1] Common to all of these works is fantasy, the unfettered imagination of the

---

[1] See chapter 2 for several common themes in *Spitballs* and Kinsella's *Shoeless Joe* and *The Iowa Baseball Confederacy.* Kinsella does not acknowledge many direct sources, and none among baseball writers. In interviews he has cited Ray Bradbury, Richard Brautigan, and Gabriel García Márquez as inspirations for his magical realism. The "sources" for *Shoeless Joe,* which he knew he wanted to write about before he had a novel in mind, were his father's recollections of Shoeless Joe Jackson; the intriguing, miniscule entry for Moonlight Graham in the *Baseball Encyclopedia,* which prompted him, like Ray Kinsella, to travel to Chisholm, Minnesota, to learn about him; an eighty-seven-year-old imposter in Iowa City (Kinsella named him Eddie Scissons) who claimed to have played for the Chicago Cubs; and a rereading of J. D. Salinger's works, where he found two characters named Kinsella. "Ah," he said on discovering that, "there's the tie-in. There's the tie-in" (*Spitball* interview, 57).

individual who harbors the dream of a better world and is willing to challenge a seemingly irresistible "reality." In its stereotyped collision of good with evil, *Shoeless Joe* also has elements of an old-fashioned American melodrama, as we shall see later.

Field of Dreams[2]

From the book's epigraph—Bobby Kennedy's signature remark that "Some men see things as they are, and say why. I dream things that never were and say why not"—to the end of the novel, man's penchant for dreaming is a main theme of *Shoeless Joe*.[3] Its fanciful plot begins when the narrator and protagonist, a kindly dreamer named Ray Kinsella,[4] hears the call of a spirit baseball announcer, "If you build it, he will come" (3),[5] and responds by creating a lush left field on his Iowa farm. Sure enough, "he" appears, Shoeless Joe Jackson. At Jackson's behest, the narrator eventually completes the park, and the rest of the banished players arrive to play game after game under the dreamy gaze of Kinsella and his family.

---

[2] The title for the enormously successful film version of *Shoeless Joe*, *Field of Dreams* (1989), was well chosen. Dreams and dreaming are an essential component of both works.

[3] Indeed, Kinsella states that his novel is "a story about the power of love and the power of dreams; it's about the ability to chase a dream and make it come true" (cited in Murray, 50).

[4] The reader must keep in mind that in referring to "Kinsella" we sometimes mean the narrator, Ray, and sometimes the author, W. P. The author rejects the notion of what he calls "the implied author syndrome," i.e., that his protagonists are in any way identical to him. He has Salinger say something to that effect: "Once and for all, *I am not Holden Caulfield*. I am an illusionist who created Holden Caulfield from my imagination" (74; W. P. Kinsella's italics). Kinsella insists that his own life is uninteresting and that newspaper stories and people he meets provide the start of his ideas. His fruitful imagination takes over from there. In *Shoeless Joe* he does use real names for his narrator's father, John Kinsella, and wife, Annie. Moreover, Ray Kinsella's views on society and religion reflect the positions of his creator. Ultimately, however, the author distances himself from his gentle creations in writing, "I am much more cynical than my characters, much angrier, I am always very conscious of the absurdity that surrounds me" (*The Thrill of the Grass*, ix).

[5] All citations from *Shoeless Joe* are from the 1983 Ballantine Books paperback edition.

The narrator realizes another dream when he induces (actually kidnaps) recluse author J. D. Salinger to join him for a Boston Red Sox game at Fenway Park. This, too, is in response to the mysterious voice, which has told Kinsella to "ease his pain" (27), caused by Salinger's unfulfilled dream of playing in New York's Polo Grounds. At the game, Salinger and Kinsella, alone among the Fenway throng, see a cryptic message on the scoreboard (a brief *Baseball Encyclopedia* entry) and hear the voice bid them "Go the distance" (79); Salinger, for his part, hears an additional message, "Fulfill the dream" (89). True to their calling, they head off for the Midwest in search of an old-time ballplayer named Archibald "Moonlight" Graham, on a journey through time that shows us people dreaming about, wishing for, seeking, and sometimes finding their heart's desire. The narrator treasures this quest as something profoundly human. The dream alone is sweet and sufficient; seeing it come true is but a wonderful bonus. "I know," he says, "that some of us, and for some reason I am one of them, get to reach out and touch our heart's desire, like a child who gets to pet the nose of an old horse, soft as satin, safe as grandfather's lap. And I know, too, that when most people reach for that heart's desire, it appears not as a horse but as a tiger, and they are rewarded with snarls, frustration, and disillusionment" (184). In seeing his park come to life, Kinsella has touched his heart's desire. As the novel progresses, the enchanted field fulfills the dreams of others as well.

Time Travel

A central quality of dreams is that they transcend time, and flying "softly across the dimensions of time" (208) is another main theme of this novel. *Shoeless Joe* does that so artfully that the time-bound reader longs to break free and take flight with Kinsella and his entourage. Just as the narrator can indulge his fantasies about the past, so the dead players can enliven the big sleep with games played far in their future. Like them, the reader is eager for the strands of blended time to create their magic tapestry. "I want," says the narrator, "whatever miracle I am party to, to prosper and grow: I want the dimensions of time that have been loosened from their foundations to entwine like a basketful of bright embroidery threads. But it seems that even for dreams, I have to work and wait. It hardly seems fair" (23). With J. D. Salinger, the reader is also a time traveler in the Hall of Fame at Cooperstown, New York, and like Moonlight Graham, an obscure outfielder who played one inning of one major league game, he floats "adrift on the sea of time" (166).

More than any other character, Graham embodies the timeless structure of this novel. Although told about his careers as an undistinguished big leaguer and a popular small-town doctor, the reader actually meets him on two different planes of past time that blend in and out of the fantastic present of the Iowa ballpark.[6] First, when in 1979 Kinsella and Salinger are in Chisholm, Minnesota, researching Graham's life there, Ray goes for a walk and imperceptibly slips back in time to the year 1955. He encounters the seventy-five-year-old Doc Graham and converses about Graham's nickname, his baseball career, his calling as a physician, and the curious nature of their meeting. Graham felt "a pulling, like there was a magnet drawing me slowly toward it. Are you a magnet, Ray Kinsella?" (118). Kinsella wonders, "Can it be that I am the one who has crossed some magical line between fantasy and reality?" (118).[7] Ray explains that he came to

---

[6] Neil Randall uses J. R. R. Tolkien's terms "Primary World" and "Secondary World" (175) to refer to the two planes of time, the former being Iowa and the latter being the phenomenon that "seems to follow Ray around" (176) and involves other people and places.

[7] Cf. *Things Invisible to See*, which depicts a line between space-time and a spiritual reality beyond it. Some people and spirits have the ability magically to transverse that line.

Chisholm to learn how the experience of coming so close to his dream, only to see it vanish, affected the doctor's life. Graham's response is one of the novel's memorable maxims: "If I'd only got to be a doctor for five minutes, now *that* would have been a tragedy. You've got to keep things in perspective" (127). At Ray's insistence, however, he does admit to a wish to bat in a major league game.

The second meeting between Graham and Kinsella illustrates anew that, as in other baseball novels, one can "take time and turn it in your hands like rubbing up a new baseball" (127). As they leave Chisholm to return to Iowa, Kinsella and Salinger pick up a hitchhiker looking for a place to play ball. It is Archie Graham, a fresh-faced youngster "crisscrossing the dimensions of time" (133), who has joined 1979 to ride to Kinsella's Iowa ballpark. When he steps on the magical field, he leaves space-time to join Joe Jackson and the White Sox. Then, when the narrator's young daughter, Karin, falls from the bleacher and chokes on a hot dog, Archie reenters 1979 to rescue her. His metamorphosis in a few lines of fantastic prose is representative of the ghostly timelessness of the entire novel:

What I see is Moonlight Graham loping in from right field, lithe, dark, athletic: the same handsome young man who played that one inning of baseball in 1905. But as he moves closer, his features begin to change, his step slows. He seems to become smaller. His baseball uniform fades away and is replaced by a black overcoat. His baseball cap is gone, supplanted by a thatch of white hair. As I watch, his glove miraculously turns into a black bag (208).

Kinsella marvels as the Doctor Graham he met in Minnesota revives his daughter in Iowa, but he wonders "how much he has sacrificed to save

Karin's life. It seems to me that he will never be able to walk onto the ball field as Moonlight Graham. He has violated some cosmic rule that I vaguely know exists, and do not even attempt to understand" (209). Having fulfilled his baseball wish of batting in the Major Leagues, Graham gladly returns through the cornfield to his medical career and his true calling.

To dwell on time as Kinsella does is fascinating, but it is also bittersweet. Revisiting the prime of an aged or dead hero or loved one reminds one of one's own mortality. Thornton Wilder demonstrates that beautifully in his classic play, *Our Town*. Reliving her twelfth birthday, Emily Webb is so overcome by the trip through time that she regrets having undertaken it. "More in wonder than in grief," she expresses what we all feel when faced with the passage of time: "I can't bear it. They're so young and beautiful. Why did they ever have to get old?" (61).

This is reminiscent of another poignant time trip taken by Roger Kahn in his baseball classic, *The Boys of Summer*. Kahn does not deal in anachronisms; rather, he contrasts the vitality of the outstanding Brooklyn Dodger teams of the early 1950s with the later lives of the heroes, after their skills have faded. Despite his obvious fascination with baseball, Kahn states that his book "is not on sports but on time and what time does to all of us."[8] The same can be said of W. P. Kinsella's work, for whom time is both the medium *and* the message. The literary medium is fanciful time travel, by virtue of which Kinsella gets to reverse Kahn's message of the human erosion process. In *Shoeless Joe*, the narrator knows his father only as a tired man, worn down by life and prematurely aged, but through the power of his imagination and the fluid nature of time, Ray Kinsella can glory in his

---

[8] From the author's comments on the book's dust jacket. Kahn, trained in English and American literature before accepting a job in sports journalism, goes on to say that "*King Lear* is on the same subject as *The Boys of Summer*, and my work differs from *Lear* in that it isn't as good."

father's promising youth and help him fulfill his dream. Likewise, we first see Moonlight Graham as an aging physician, then as a youth living out his baseball wish.

Familial Love

As much as it is a book about dreams and time, *Shoeless Joe* is also a love story (cf. note 33), celebrating the narrator's love of life and his desire to savor each day of it. Prominent among his many loves are his family and, of course, the sport of baseball. Baseball, because it resists the ravages of time, prolongs the life the author seeks to enjoy. "I don't have to tell you," he has Salinger say, "that the only constant through all the years has been baseball. America has been erased like a blackboard, only to be rebuilt and then erased again. But baseball has marked time while America has rolled by like a procession of steamrollers" (213). Baseball is also a rich, beautiful, and subtle game whose essence is captured by Kinsella in several lyrical passages that rival the charm of any of baseball's noted poets.

The narrator's family is the other main subject of the love story. Explaining the genesis of his love for his wife and the farm they inhabit, Kinsella states, "I came to Iowa to study, one of the thousands of faceless students who pass through large universities, but I fell in love with the state. Fell in love with the land, the people, the sky, the cornfields, and Annie.... It was Annie who got me to buy [the farm]" (9). His wife also approves of the fantastic venture with his ballpark, despite its putting them behind in their mortgage payments. Her incredible patience and abiding love give Kinsella the strength to pursue his dream in the face of ridicule. "'Whatever happens, I'm with you, Champ,' she says, and erases my anxiety with her soft, sweet love" (184).[9]

Despite her limited understanding of baseball, Annie is attuned to the growing magic on the farm, and it is she who first discovers the presence of Shoeless Joe Jackson on the lovingly prepared left field. Daughter Karin also believes in her father and is often the first to announce the descent of magic on the field.[10] (Ray's long-dead father and long-lost twin brother appear later as the family story becomes one of reunion and reconciliation.) In their shared experiences on the rickety bleacher, Ray, Annie, and Karin are molded into an American family that is living its dream, and they long to share it with others.

Melodrama

Their idyll is threatened by meddling members of Annie's family, the "bad guys," the chief nemesis among whom is brother Mark. (The other brothers are named—uh-oh—Matthew, Luke, and John. Their overtly pious mother is a source of irritation for Kinsella, but she is not a major character in the novel.) Ray Kinsella states that Mark "has always looked to me like the villain from a nineteenth-century melodrama" (61). He also "has a wine-colored mustache that turns up wickedly at each corner, apparently of its own accord. I've never seen him twirl the mustache like a genuine villain, but I'm sure he will one day" (61).

---

[9] The narrator Kinsella enjoys describing the physical charms of Annie, who is the prototype of several similar women found in the collected short stories of the author Kinsella called *The Thrill of the Grass* and in the novel *The Iowa Baseball Confederacy*. With her red hair, green eyes, freckles, and sensuous mouth, she prefigures Sunny, Nursie, Rose, Delly, and Sarah in their electric attraction for Kinsella's protagonists.

[10] Dave and Paul Healy's fine analysis of the mythic significance of a ball field (infield = local farm, outfield = frontier) sees the players as beginning an "archetypal journey with each trip to the plate." Citing historian David Noble's representation of the American dream, they write that the players' "object is to leave home, then, like Odysseus, successfully navigate their way through hostile territory, and finally return as conquering heroes" (34).

Mark's business partner is an accountant named Bluestein, "a squat little man with terminal five o'clock shadow and shifty eyes" (62). The two men are local business tycoons who buy up family farms for a giant agricultural concern. "Mark, Bluestein and their associates have a sinister master plan for the whole area, and our little quarter-section is like a fly backstroking in their crab bisque" (164). In threatening to foreclose on Kinsella's farm, where the mortgage payments are in arrears, they represent sinister forces conspiring to crush the American dream. Ray Kinsella thrives on fantasy, but Mark tells him, "You're going to have to face the facts" (62). A wellspring of the narrator's life is his beloved cornfield baseball park, but Mark and Bluestein[11] plan to bulldoze the bleacher and plow the diamond under as soon as they gain control.

The melodramatic menace introduced in the first half of the novel is resumed near the end. Again the stereotypical villains close in on the innocents. Kinsella bravely resists the takeover effort, fighting not only for himself but for other downtrodden dreamers. "If I can hold my land," he reasons, "remain free, it could begin a chain reaction that, like opening a row of cages in a zoo, would free half of Johnson County, Iowa, from this computer-farming syndicate" (164). In preserving the ghostly park, Ray is also prolonging the dream of the Unlucky Eight, whose careers were terminated—many say unjustly—by the dictatorial baseball commissioner, Judge Kenesaw Mountain Landis. "What would happen to all of you," Kinsella asks, "if this ballpark is razed, leveled, planted in corn?" (185). They give no

---

[11] The name and character of Bluestein suggest several sinister parallels. The first part of the name calls to mind the archvillain Bluebeard; the second half echoes Arnold Rothstein, the notorious gambler who "fixed" the 1919 World Series, which led to Joe Jackson's banishment from baseball. This is reinforced by the description of Bluestein's suit that "makes him look like a gangster" (203). Finally, there is Meyer Wolfsheim, the character in Scott Fitzgerald's novel *The Great Gatsby*, himself a take-off on Rothstein. W. P. Kinsella names *The Great Gatsby* as one of two books he would own if he could keep no other. The other is *In Watermelon Sugar*, by Richard Brautigan.

answer, but as the players "exchange knowing glances" (185), the reader presumes that they would return to the limbo from which they came.

The final act of the melodrama, true to the clichéd genre, finds the villains approaching the ball field with a court order in one hand and a sparkling ax in the other. The innocent heroine Annie scuffles with her brother while Bluestein moves in with the ax, "his malevolent black eyes coming close to smiling" (203). But it is the park, not Annie, that he wants: "We're going to knock down that eyesore of a fence and that pile of rubble you call a bleacher" (203). Kinsella, the gentle hero, can tolerate no more and brandishes a gun to stop the villains. After a prolonged standoff, the tension is broken only when daughter Karin takes a hard fall down the bleacher and begins to convulse as she chokes on a hot dog. General concern for her well-being and relief at her rescue by Doc Graham defuse the crisis. Only then do we learn that the suddenly compassionate Bluestein is named Abner (alias Doubleday?), and the novel moves past the family conflict to its conclusion as J. D. Salinger is invited to join the players after the game. Much to the dismay of the jealous Ray Kinsella, Salinger is "raptured"[12] beyond the centerfield fence, and the fulfillment of his dream continues.

Religious Imagery

The frequency (three dozen or so) of concepts such as "rapture" gives *Shoeless Joe* an unmistakably religious dimension. Like Sister Timothy in *Spitballs and Holy Water*, the narrator, Ray Kinsella, hears a voice and acts in obedience to it. He is also given two visions: "the vision of the baseball park...and a vision within the vision: one of Shoeless Joe Jackson playing

---

[12] The word "rapture," though not found in the Bible, is used by some Christians to denote a direct transporting of believers to heaven as described in the New Testament. The term is also found in *The Iowa Baseball Confederacy* and is depicted in Kinsella's short story "Frank Pierce, Iowa."

left field" (6). Ray also speaks of digging his first garden on the rich Iowa farmland as an "epiphany...an experience of religious significance" (14). He takes issue with the fundamentalist religion of his wife's family[13] and offers in its place a quasi-religious celebration of life: dreams, books, green grass, love, immortality, and the sum of these things, "the great god Baseball" (6). Other religious terms, such as "ritual," "sacrament," "sign," "omen," "revelation," "congregation," "miracle," "penance," and "faith" are regularly used to convey the profound impact of baseball on its followers and its ability to give new life to its followers. At the Hall of Fame, Kinsella touches one of the "relics" with "reverence...as if I were in a basilica, reaching out tentatively to finger the face of a holy statue" (94). An empty ballpark, he tells us, is "both eerie and holy.... A ballpark at night is more like a church than a church" (94).

The concept of a "chosen" people[14] is an especially prominent one in *Shoeless Joe*, which combined with the activities at the cornfield ballpark

---

[13] This, too, is a biographical detail. Kinsella states that he was an agnostic until he met his future wife's fundamentalist family and friends, and a confirmed atheist thereafter (Murray 40).

[14] *Shoeless Joe*'s emphasis on the concept of "chosenness" is significant, for it links the novel with the foundational American religion, Puritanism. As Catherine Albanese explains, "the Puritans came to see themselves as the true chosen people from an almost-chosen England.... First of all, they were to be an *example* for all the world to see—a society of God's elect, in which righteousness had triumphed and sin would reign no more. Secondly, they had a *mission* to spread the message and the meaning of their gospel to others" (286; her emphasis). In building his park, Ray Kinsella, the baseball purist, or Puritan, has created an example for the world to see, and in evangelizing Salinger, Richard, and Eddie, he is fulfilling his mission of spreading the baseball gospel.

Albanese points out that millennialism is another characteristic of Puritanism that appears repeatedly in American culture. "Sometimes it has been the dominating millennialism which takes its cue from visions of the final battle when good will triumph over evil. Other times it has been the innocent millennialism which seeks to make utopia in the uncorrupted landscape" (341). This, too, suggests the religious qualities of *Shoeless Joe*. Good and evil struggle in Kinsella's melodrama and in the ghostly allegory transpiring on the field, which itself epitomizes "utopia in the uncorrupted landscape."

Joseph L. Price calls the messages that Ray Kinsella receives pre-millennial: "The pre-millennial eschatology is oriented toward preparing for the Second Coming, toward initiating the Kingdom of God through some form of believers' communities, toward persevering through the process of expectation: All of these elements lie at the heart of the revelation, expectation, and fulfillment that generate the hope and purpose of the true believers in *Field of Dreams*" ("Exit Laughing," 6).

makes the novel something of a religious allegory.[15] The athletes who make the Major Leagues are "chosen"; so too are the spectators who believe sufficiently in the divine nature of the game that their eyes are opened to its beauty. For the players, who presumably have repented of their World Series sins, the cornfield park offers a reprieve from the "Devil," as Judge Landis is called in the novel. The park grants them a taste of heaven, and indeed Joe Jackson asks if that is where he is. The realm beyond the fence, to which the players retire after each game, can be seen either as a hell—i.e., a place with no baseball—or a limbo or purgatory from which they have only limited access to baseball heaven. When asked about their existence beyond the centerfield fence, the players are reluctant to comment. "We sleep," is all they say. "And wait…. And dream" (186).

The ballpark is also a kind of heaven for the mortals on earth, i.e., on the bleacher. If they believe, it is their promise of salvation, an escape from the mundane reality with which they struggle. There is also a self-sacrificing "savior" in *Shoeless Joe*: Doc Graham not only saves Kinsella's choking daughter but gives up his own baseball life by moving from one dimension of time to another.

But who chooses the "chosen," and why? Salinger implies that it is the spirit players: "there must be a reason for them to choose me, just as there was a reason for them to choose you, and Iowa, and this farm" (222). In each case, the "reason" matches the circumstances: Ray's desire to draw closer to his father; the father's ambition to play in the big leagues; Salinger's

---

[15] Linda S. Joffe doesn't analyze *Shoeless Joe* as an allegory, but she does touch on many of the same points as my analysis in comparing the religious metaphors in the novel and the film, *Field of Dreams*. Rebecca Easton does discuss *Shoeless Joe* as an allegory, but, as indicated above, of the power of the creative imagination for fiction writers.

longing to play in the Polo Grounds (he wonders if that New York ballpark "might just be floating around out there" [223]); Graham's wish to bat against big leaguers. Once he himself is chosen, however, Kinsella becomes a major prophet[16] of baseball, an evangelist who heeds the call of the spirit announcer and converts many whom he touches.[17]

His twin brother, Richard, is something of a case study of a believer who comes to faith in stages. At first, he mocks the idea that Ray and his family see anything beyond a strange ballpark cut into the corn. Then he acknowledges that something special exists but wonders why *he* can't see. Desperate to experience what others do, he pleads, "Ray, teach me how to see" (201), but still without success. Only when Richard accompanies Ray onto the field after a game and hears him address their father does the breakthrough come. Rather than scales, Kinsella uses the image of gauze that must fall, or be removed, from his brother's eyes, as Ray and Salinger tell him of the wonders of the game. "I feel as if I am watching a war movie in which a nurse is removing the last feet of white bandage from a soldier's eyes. Will he see?" (214). Like blind Bartimaeus healed by Jesus, he will. Like Paul in Damascus, he does. "'It's true' says Richard, air exploding from his lungs" (214).

---

[16] I agree with Charles Franklin Beach that Ray is above all a prophet or priest in the "religion" of baseball and that equating him with Jesus or Moses is an incomplete analogy, despite his role as a leader in the "resurrection" of the dead ballplayers (89). One need not establish an exact correspondence to a particular figure; it suffices to say that Ray proclaims the word like a faithful prophet, mediates like a priest, and seeks to convert others like an evangelist.

[17] A splendid passage in which Kinsella considers how he will "convert" Salinger concludes with the image of himself as a bottle of blood administering a transfusion: "I'll pierce a vein and feed him the sounds, smells, and sights of baseball until he tingles with the same magic that enchants me" (34).

Ray Kinsella is careful to acknowledge that while he chooses others, it is only done through the guidance of a higher power:[18] "I chose Jerry, Moonlight, and Eddie. But it wasn't exactly my own doing. It was like walking out in front of a full grandstand, the breath of thirty thousand faces on me, the throng clapping, cheering, stomping, whistling, reaching out to be chosen; but it was also like having my hand guided to pick out the *right* ones" (173). It seems, therefore, that a force far beyond man is guiding his destiny, but what is that force?

In the travesty of a religious revival found near the end of the novel, Kinsella implies that "the great god Baseball" (6) is that force.[19] "Looking for all the world like an Old Testament prophet on the side of a mountain," it is old Eddie Scissons who proclaims the baseball gospel from Kinsella's bleacher. "The word of salvation is baseball within you, and let it dwell within you richly.... The word of baseball is spirit and it is life.... Praise the name of baseball. The word will set captives free. The word will open the eyes of the blind" (191-93). Indeed, the ability to see—natural for some, hard and unnatural for others like Richard—is the mark of the believer.

If the god of Kinsella's theology is Baseball, then the divine force that works in people's lives and brings them to faith is "magic."[20] There are

---

[18] There is a biblical passage, 1 Chronicles 28:9-10, that could be the model for Kinsella's call by a higher power. David is advising his son, Solomon, of the need to devote himself to God's service by building the temple. "If you seek him, he will be found by you," says David, which sounds like Ray Kinsella's mandate, "If you build it, he will come." "It" refers to the park, a great temple that Kinsella, like Solomon, has been chosen to construct. "Consider now, for the Lord has chosen you to build a temple as a sanctuary. Be strong and do the work."

[19] In a discussion with Don Murray about hero worship, Kinsella reveals how he may have arrived at the inspired phrase that serves as the title for this book: "It seems to me that baseball is the hero that we worship rather than the individual players who make up the game" (48), i.e., the great god Baseball.

[20] As noted above, W. P. Kinsella, though he masterfully creates literary magic, rejects any notion of transcendence. In his introduction to his collection of stories, *The Thrill of the Grass*, he writes, "The very idea is ludicrous.... I am a realist. There are no gods. There is no magic" (xi). Thus, we must, as with most of the fanciful baseball novels that employ religious themes, suspend disbelief as we enter their magic kingdom.

some two dozen references to magic in *Shoeless Joe*, and if one substitutes for it a form of the word "spirit"—spiritual, spirit-filled, the spirit of God, the Holy Spirit—one completes the theological construct that connects the great god Baseball with his chosen people. As opposed to the fearsome power of voodoo and witch doctors, such as is found in *The Seventh Babe*, *Things Invisible to See*, and *Havana Heat*, Kinsella's magic is gentle. Moreover, the verbs that describe it are scarcely in the passive voice, with an insistent human agent conjuring it up with chants, potions, and talismans. Instead, Kinsella depicts magic with active verbs, indicating that it comes of its own accord. Before Joe Jackson's first appearance on the Iowa left field, the magic "*builds* like a gathering storm." Ray Kinsella feels it "*drawing* closer, *hovering* somewhere out in the night like a zeppelin, silky and silent, *floating* like the moon until the time is right" (11); "Annie senses that magic is about to *happen*" (11). Later, the magic "*unfolds*" (not *is* unfolded; 154), "*lowered* [not *was* lowered] onto and around my ballpark" (191), and "*drew*" (not *was* drawn; 195; my italics).

When Salinger asks for a definition of the ballpark magic, Kinsella answers not with theology, but in what we might call cosmic terms about a loving deity outside of space-time who delights in granting his chosen ones their heart's desire. "It's the place and the time. The right place and right time. Iowa is the right place, and the time is right, too—a time when all the cosmic tumblers have clicked into place and the universe opens up for a few seconds, or hours, and shows you what is possible" (84).

The religious component of *Shoeless Joe* does far more than simply tweak the almost religious devotion of true baseball fans. It nurtures the blessings that Ray Kinsella already enjoys with his wife and daughter, and now, as the magic enfolds them, wants to talk of with "the catcher"—his father—and his brother: "love, and family, and life, and beauty, and friendship, and sharing." (215). As a vehicle for experiencing these joys, baseball is exquisite, and this novel may indeed open the eyes of those who are blind to the charms of the game. For those whose eyes are already open, it is not only a visual treat but one that will caress all of their senses.

Inning 5:

The Baseball Messiah:
Christy Mathewson and *The Celebrant*

The Celebrant, the only novel published by its author, Eric Rolfe Greenberg, has been praised by no less an authority than W. P. Kinsella, the award-winning author of *Shoeless Joe* and *The Iowa Baseball Confederacy*, as "simply the best baseball novel ever written." I had never heard of *The Celebrant*, but Kinsella's endorsement on the book's front cover was all I needed to buy it. Once again, my teacher/librarian instincts moved me immediately to talk and write about this little-known gem of a novel. The richness that characterizes it is created by Greenberg's portrayal of and commentary on the transience of human existence, suggested initially by the epigraph, a quotation from the Prologue to Shakespeare's *Henry VIII*:

> Be sad, as we would make ye. Think ye se
> The very persons of our noble story
> As they were living. Think you see them great,
> And follow'd with the general throng, and sweat
> Of thousand friends. Then, in a moment, see
> How soon this mightiness meets misery.

Transience is further illustrated at the novel's end by the demise of the narrator's idol, Christy Mathewson, the first great baseball legend. Thus, immortality is contrasted with mortality, glory with defeat, mightiness with misery, and the fortunate reader is privy to the hot breath of greatness and the death rattle of mortality.

Between the foreground of an exciting baseball story and the background mural of transient human glories lie several other engaging topics in *The Celebrant*: a colorful retelling of New York and American history, the role of baseball in the social integration of immigrants, the rise and fall of business interests, the loss of innocence with the 1919 Black Sox scandal, and an artful religious allegory focusing on Mathewson as messiah. All of these themes are important components of Greenberg's novel, and although this chapter will touch briefly on several of them, it will concentrate on the last, religion.

Recreating the Past

Perhaps the real genius of this book is that it so deftly transports us to the early years of the twentieth century. There is no awkward, self-conscious sense of constructing what we in the twentieth-first century *think* life must have been like then. Rather, as one sits on the trains, wanders through the hotel lobbies, and crouches with the crowd atop Coogan's Bluff to peer down on the Giants at their Polo Grounds, one genuinely has the sense of breathing the same air as Mathewson and McGraw.

This is understandable, when one considers Greenberg's acknowledged sources, but the sources do not detract at all from his considerable skill in synthesizing them in graceful and moving prose. Greenberg reconstructed the details of many games by consulting the reportage of the *New York Times*, and he appears to have assimilated the journalistic speech of the day. He also acknowledges the inspiration of Eliot Asinof's *Eight Men Out*, Joseph Durso's *The Days of Mr. McGraw*, and Lawrence Ritter's *The Glory of Their Times*. (Greenberg does not include in his acknowledgments Christy Mathewson's *Pitching in a Pinch*, ghostwritten in the lingo of the century's first decades by sports journalist John Wheeler, but he does mention it in the text.)

The Glory of Their Times (another work that has been termed the best baseball book ever) was likely the key source for Greenberg, for it relives the early days of twentieth-century baseball in taped interviews with the men who played it.[1] Several participants in games recreated in *The Celebrant* tell, as Lawrence Ritter writes in his preface, "not only about what it was like to be a baseball player in the early days, but also about what it was like just to be alive then [xvii]. …And in recalling those days, in remembering what their teammates and their opponents were like, in reminiscing about their victories and their defeats, they re-create with dramatic impact the sights and sounds, the vigor and the vitality, of an era that can never return" (xvi). But in a magical way that characterizes the best of writing, the era *does* return in *The Celebrant*.

---

[1] As with *The Celebrant*, Ritter's book is about more than baseball. As cited in the introduction above, it is, he writes, about human aspirations and the struggles of our mortal existence.

Greenberg's intimacy with a bygone era enriches our view not only of baseball and New York but also of the immigrant experience as fictionally related through the Russian-Jewish family of the narrator, Yakov Kapinsky, alias Jackie Kapp. Baseball, it turns out, is a catalyst to the assimilation and success of his family, first gaining Jackie acceptance as a pretty fair sandlot pitcher, then converting the popularity of Mathewson and McGraw to wealth in the Kapps' jewelry business that produces elegant championship rings.

Jackie's time on the ball field had molded him into an American: "First by imitation, then by practice, we learned the game and the ways of the boys who played it, the angle of their caps, the intonations of their curses and encouragements. Our accents disappeared, our strides became quick and confident" (12). However, Jackie's dreams of a professional career conflict with the dreams of his family for success in the New World: "All the pressure of a family's traditions, hopes, and plans pressed down upon me…but though my parents came to believe that I'd actually be paid to play ball the issue went far deeper than money. We had not crossed the ocean to find disgraceful employment" (14).

Jackie Kapp accedes to his father's pressure and joins the family firm as an artist, designing jewelry, but baseball continues to facilitate the acculturation of the Kapps. Brother Eli is fond of entertaining business clients at the ballpark—"so refreshing, so American" (17)—and Jackie is brought along to impress the clients with his knowledge of the game and to give Eli information with which to support his growing fondness for gambling. Eli "required a wager to excite his interest, whereas for me the game was all" (15).

Baseball—and specifically the poise and prowess of the superb Giants pitcher Christy Mathewson—provides Jackie an artistic inspiration that leads to lucrative contracts and extensive publicity for the growing jewelry firm. This moves the Kapps one step farther from their roots when control of the business is assumed by the youngest brother, Arthur: "Alone of us all he was American born and accustomed to the spoiling riches of the New World" (103).[2] The firm prospers under Arthur's leadership, who sees his mandate as that of a protector—"Did Uncle Sid build all this so that the family could live well for two generations and then slowly sink back from whence we came?" (227)—and a leader, away from a dying Continent and into the exciting new frontier: "This is America's hour. If we stay out of dying Europe's wars and build our own empire it can last a thousand years! There are dukedoms to be won, family fortunes to last an eternity!" (228).

Jackie is not so quick to follow Arthur's lead, not because he wishes to cling to Europe and his Russian roots (though he does enjoy travel to the Continent and relishes the international flavor of New York's ethnic neighborhoods), but because he fears that becoming fully American will threaten his identity as a Jew. The menacing anti-Semitic remarks of two Giants players continue to haunt Kapp, though Eli is quick to excuse and forget them. With age, Jackie, almost alone among his family, seeks solace and security in his faith, especially after the death of his daughter.

As the narrator looks back on his life, he reflects on the game of baseball as an almost magical tie to youth: "There is," he writes, "nothing that can so delight the heart as being a boy again, and there is no better transport to that happy past than a victory in a boy's game" (135). This is hardly a new insight for baseball fans, but it is significant for the novel's wistful look at our mortality and at the significance in the novel of Christy Mathewson. The pitcher towers above his contemporaries as the book's

---

[2] The youngest Kapp is called "King Arthur" by his brothers, a "regent" with Collegiate Jewelers as his "realm" (250). There are several other references with a medieval ring—e.g., Mathewson as "Galahad" (108) and a "knight errant" (167), the players as "knights who bear the city's emblem on their breasts" (250; cf. *The Natural*)—but otherwise that motif is not prominent in the novel.

central figure and shares something of a symbiotic relationship with the narrator. "I watched Mathewson," Kapp writes after giving up his baseball dream to enter the family business, "and he became my youth [26]. ...He was everything I was not [29]. ...I seemed to live within him [94]." As designer of the family's fine jewelry, Kapp draws much of his inspiration from the greatness of Mathewson, yet he respectfully keeps his distance. It is this respect that appeals to the pitcher and keeps drawing him back to Kapp, even after prolonged absences. "You were made for one another," Arthur Kapp tells his brother Jackie. "You think he's a kind of god, and I suspect that he shares your belief" (178). Indeed, Mathewson does assume the nature and proportions of deity in the novel.

Religious Allusions

Dozens of religious images and allusions enrich the novel, elevating baseball to a sacred realm, within which something of a passion play is acted out, with Mathewson assuming the role of the suffering—and ultimately avenging—messiah. The Polo Grounds is "a secular house of worship" (95), where the crowds seek to "lay hands upon the heroes" (76). For Jackie, the field itself is akin to sacred space: "It's a player's place, not mine. I never earned my way, and I'd feel it cheating to steal onto the field in the midst of a mob" (152). The players share a "sacred mystery" (232), their deeds are recorded in the "sacred scrolls" (250) of *The Sporting News* (long known as "The Bible of Baseball"), and the fans "praise their favorites with hallelujahs" (239). Those unfortunate players who fall out of favor, however, such as "Bonehead" Fred Merkle, the scapegoat in the 1908 loss to the Cubs, suffer "crucifixion" (150).

The forceful leader of the Giants, John McGraw, appears initially as a minor deity himself. There is reference to his "advent" (50) and to the "respectful attention" of the players, when, in a gesture of praise, concessionaire Harry M. Stevens "stretched his arms skyward and cried out the name of McGraw" (61). McGraw is "worshipped" (79) by the mob on Coogan's Bluff, but not by Jackie Kapp, who sees him more as a false god, competing with Mathewson, whom he admits to worshiping from afar. It vexes him that the cultured Mathewson can speak so highly of the profane field manager. Matty praises McGraw's virtues and inspiration and states, "When I learned that he was to manage the club I felt I'd found salvation" (91). And he is anxious to follow his leader "through the fire" (91) and into the "Armegeddon that will commence in the second week of October" (92). But although some mistake John McGraw for the messiah, he is more a John the Baptist, preparing the way and proclaiming the greatness of the one who will follow. Though Matty's modesty initially prevents him from assuming the role of messiah, he eventually accepts that identity in unmistakable terms.

Despite his brother Eli's observation that Mathewson is "only flesh and blood" (37), Jackie treats the Giants pitcher with the awe and reverence normally reserved for deity. However, because Jackie routinely uses terms that have both a secular and a sacred meaning, the deification of Mathewson emerges only gradually and subtly. His pitches are "pure" (59), his performance "perfect" (81, 108). He is the acknowledged "master" (94, 130) who has become an "icon" (111), a "prince among the people" (111), wearing a "crown" (121). On the mound before a crucial game, the pitcher has "communion" (129) and "private devotions" (135), while Jackie, his fondest admirer, is a "witness" to his greatness, yearning "to confess my faith and share his glory" (135).

Before establishing Mathewson as a messiah, Jackie portrays the pitcher's extraordinary nature by contrasting him with the rough, profane McGraw, who, as we have seen, is only briefly mistaken for a savior, and with Joe McGinnity, the Giants' other star pitcher. Where Mathewson is the "pure pitcher," McGinnity, nicknamed "Iron Man," is the "primitive thrower" (59). The durable hurler is as "unsubtle as the steam locomotives that brought up more and more eager spectators" (47). In victory he is "a mighty machine...a driving piston" (77), in defeat "a mechanical contraption" (94).

Mathewson, on the other hand, is purity and subtlety. The power of his body suggests to Jackie the marble statuary of the classic Greek athletes, and were he a sculptor, he "would have carved Mathewson's statue for the spire of a cathedral" (167). As his admiration for Mathewson's figure and performance transcends the secular and the professional, it becomes religious reverence.

Only once does the narrator bring himself to agree with his brother's assessment of Mathewson as a mere mortal: "I thought that he would order time to stand still, leaving him suspended for eternity in his pose, at this breath, but only gods and artists can stop time. Mathewson had to pitch, erasing this moment, bringing on the next" (99). Otherwise, Kapp defines the pitcher in terms of his own devotion and Matty's striking messianic pronouncements at the end. Just as he respects the sacred space of the playing field, so Kapp keeps his distance from the person of Mathewson. He is content to be, as Eli called him, "a worshipper from afar" (42, 82), a heresy only briefly questioned; it is, after all, "a very American heresy" (42).

Jackie's worship of Mathewson provides the inspiration for his craft of jewelry design—his "offering" (66)—until 1912, in the fourth of the novel's five chapters. At that point he realizes that he, like Mathewson's ghostwriter John Wheeler, was "exploiting rather than glorifying the hero. I scanned my current work, and I was ashamed; I realized that I needed new inspiration and could not look to Mathewson to provide it" (175). Jackie resolves not to visit the Polo Grounds that year.

The agent for Kapp's new and heightened understanding of Mathewson is the journalist, Hugh Fullerton. In delivering a message from the pitcher before the final game of the 1912 World Series, Fullerton is shocked to learn of the limited personal contact between Matty and Kapp, for Matty had described their relationship as intimate. It was he who called Jackie "the celebrant of his works" (195). Once again, a key term (here, of course, the book's title) has two levels of meaning: the raucous fan celebrating victory and the worshiper presenting a religious tribute, as a priest celebrating the Mass. Mathewson understands the nature of Jackie's art and concludes his message, "I pray that I shall give you cause for celebration" (195).

Fullerton counts himself among the celebrants of Mathewson's works but ascribes a less than pure motive to their tributes: "We make the greatest demands. Every time he pitches I find myself hoping for the most extraordinary achievement, for my immortality lies in his…. I want him to throw a no-hit game tomorrow, not for his sake but for mine. And don't you want the same, so you can cover him in glory? We're the worms that eat at the bodies of the great" (196). Fullerton defines here the deity of Christy Mathewson: the immortal pitcher is himself the source of others' immortality. Fullerton's effusive colleague Wheeler had said much the same: "No writer since the author of the Gospels had borne a greater responsibility" (175).

If Mathewson is deity and journalists and artists his celebrants, then Jackie, says Fullerton, is "the high priest…the celebrant-in-chief" (196). The journalist questions Jackie's motives for staying away from the ballpark. Had the pressure of having to equal in art what Mathewson had achieved on the field overcome him? Did he secretly wish for Matty to fail and relieve him of his burden? "I can't think it" (197), says Kapp, but he begins to reevaluate his relationship to the great pitcher.

Fullerton concludes his visit to Kapp by referring to the tormented Mathewson on the eve of an important game, as "in Gethsemane" (197). The expectations of his manager, McGraw, with whom he has just quarreled, of his fans and celebrants, and his business associates (the Kapps' jewelry firm, which he endorses commercially) create the enormous pressure and doubt that Fullerton calls his Gethsemane, the garden where Christ on the eve of his crucifixion agonized over the nature of his mission and the need to suffer and die for mankind's salvation.

Matty as Messiah

The last quarter of the novel depicts Mathewson neither as a Greek god nor as a deified folk hero, but as a suffering, atoning, and ultimately punishing Christ. The messianic allusions abound. "The man on the mound," like Christ at his passion, "was never so alone" (201). He throws pitches of the "purest form" (201), is buoyant with "new life" (203), and hopes "to resurrect the glory" (207) of his team, champions seven years before, and the joy of his admirers. This time, however, his mission is thwarted. Catastrophe strikes in the form of a dropped fly ball by Fred Snodgrass and an untouched foul pop, and the Giants lose the 1912 series in the tenth inning of the seventh game. Like Jesus, "Mathewson wept" (210).

After touching on the last few years of Matty's playing career—the Giants never did regain the world's championship—the First World War, and the continued expansion of the Kapps' business, the novel concludes with the "Black Sox" betting scandal of the 1919 World Series and Mathewson's search for the ultimate purpose of his life. In the book's climactic scene, Jackie visits an ailing Mathewson to inquire about this reaction to the tainted series.[3] Matty reproaches himself for his indecision and false starts before settling assuredly into the role of messiah. Having once achieved perfection on the diamond, he sought to recapture it as a player, but his teammates knew they "were fated to lose" (262). Attempting to "regain the pinnacle" (262) as a manager was also not his role: he was no McGraw and was unable to keep his Cincinnati team from consorting with gamblers. "In contrition for his sins" (222), i.e., not having detected the gambling, Mathewson joined the Army, ready to sacrifice himself in the Great War, where he was seriously injured in a poison gas exercise. "Yet once more I mistook the lesson, I thought my fate was to die in war, under the banner of my country. I sought it out, but even there I was denied; when I awoke in the hospital I wept to be alive. What was my purpose?" (262)

In his struggle to uncover and fulfill a preordained purpose, Matty once again suggests Christ in Gethsemane: "I'd achieved the perfection you celebrated in stone. Then followed doubt, confusion, failure, and finally betrayal" (262). Now, however, he firmly accepts his role as sacrifice and ultimate judge: "Then followed my death, for it was death, in the explosion and the pain. And then I rose from that death. I walked among the people as of old, and finally, finally, I came to sit in judgment of those I'd walked among, to root out their sin and damn them for it…and when the corrupters are counting their gains I shall spring upon them and drive them from the temple!" (262)

Once again Greenberg uses a key word, "judge," with several shades of meaning. Matty, it could be said, is at the 1919 World Series simply to determine or "judge" if it is being played honestly. He and the journalists in the

---

[3] Kapp visits Mathewson in room 336 of the Congress Hotel. The number may represent Christ's age at his crucifixion, thirty-three, joined with a six for Matty's nickname, "Big Six."

press box are referred to as "jurists" (250), and it is Matty's "judgment" (253) that matters to Jackie. When Hugh Fullerton asks rhetorically, "Who's to judge?" Jackie responds literally, "Mathewson" (256).

Gambling and the deliberate losing of games are here the equivalent of the fall of man and the moneychangers in the temple. Christ's—*Christy's*—pronouncements that they will be punished are fulfilled when eight members of the losing Chicago team are banished from the game for life. The sentence is pronounced by another "judge," the new commissioner of baseball, Judge Kenesaw Mountain Landis.

Before leaving the desperately ill Mathewson, Jackie Kapp must decide whether to cover the doomed bets of brother Eli, who has wagered a fortune on the series, or to heed Christy's final messianic injunction to him: "Do you still doubt what you must do now? Do you, my celebrant? …Think of this: they diced for His robe while He suffered on the cross. Will you do that, while I lay dying? No, you will not" (263). Jackie, true to his master, calls off all of his bets and returns to New York with "the image of guiltless Mathewson in agony" (263). Eli is ruined and commits a bizarre suicide by driving a new Chalmers automobile over the jagged cliffside of Coogan's Bluff to a flaming death against the walls of the Polo Grounds.

The final, cryptic words of the novel sum up the unique symbiosis of artist and god, celebrant and messiah. "It was my happiness," writes Jackie after Mathewson's death, "to celebrate that perfection; in his age and suffering he would accept that vision of my youth, entwine it with his own hard faith, and end in madness. Eli, Eli!" (269). The cry of his brother's name echoes Christ's cry from the cross—"Eloi, Eloi—My God, my God!" Matty and Eli, the master and the brother, are both gone. Jackie Kapp and the reader are left with the haunting sense of having witnessed, in the words of the novel's epigraph, "How soon this mightiness meets misery."

Inning 6:

Cosmic Baseball for Life and Death:
Things Invisible to See

While yet a boy I sought for ghosts, and sped
Through many a listening chamber, cave and ruin,
And starlit wood, with fearful steps pursuing
Hopes of high talk with the departed dead.1
—Percy Shelley

Structure and Style

"In Paradise, on the banks of the River of Time, the Lord of the Universe is playing ball with His archangels" (3). What an opening sentence! It immediately qualifies Nancy Willard's novel for inclusion in this

---

[1] From Shelley's poem "A Hymn to Intellectual Beauty," and given by Willard in her collection of essays called *Telling Time* (21). Willard explains that Shelley did not wish to commune with terrible ghosts but with "the guardian spirits of traditional fairy tales" (35), and so indeed does she portray hers.

study. In fact, Willard has created a sensational opening page that demonstrates her highly imaginative style and constructs the loom on which she will weave a tapestry of varied spiritual threads. *Things Invisible to See* (the title, taken from a John Donne poem, suggests the magical[2] quality of the story) may have fewer pages of baseball action than any of our other novels, but the great game frames the entire book, beginning with God playing ball in heaven and ending with a three-inning showdown between the living and the dead.

In between, Willard introduces many other spiritual forces, which, she suggests, constantly infiltrate our existence in space-time. At first reading, the various spiritual threads and plot lines, intersecting and separating again, may seem confusing, but when we willingly suspend disbelief and accept the characters on their own terms, we are rewarded with a stimulating, imaginative, often poetic read. Then, when we once understand the complex correspondence between the novel's form and content, it becomes evident that *Things* is an overlooked star in the galaxy of modern baseball fiction.

Things Invisible to See consists of 260 pages in 34 chapters, each titled with a quote from within the chapter. Some of the chapters are written in a unique form of the day—World War II news bulletins and air-speeded V-mail—and some dialogues are rendered in italics to indicate that they are spoken by disembodied beings. Within the text, varied spiritual forms (God in heaven, kindly ancestor spirits, spiritualist folk healers, the personification of death) are expressed in different narrative forms (descriptions of

---

[2] Asked pointblank by an interviewer, "Do you believe in magic?" Willard answered only, "I believe things happen that we can't explain" ("Interview with Nancy Willard," video, 1991). Asked if she wished she could perform magic, she replied affirmatively. In fact, she writes as if she does believe in magic, which gives her magical realism its punch.

everyday life, powerful dreams, italicized conversations with spirits, a ball game between the living and the dead). The prominent spiritual figures who connect the real-world portrayal of human life with forces outside of space-time are central to the novel, expressing both its form and content. Therefore, to understand better the magical world created by the author and the spiritual reality she wishes to depict, we will examine some of these characters in detail. To aid this process, we include as an appendix to this chapter a chart outlining the novel's complex narrative structure.

Baseball is a vital agent in the novel, but at the book's core are the strange spiritual encounters reported by the author's family and explained in her collection of essays titled *Telling Time* (36-39). When she came to write of ghosts herself, "they were friendly to the living and gave to the everyday a spiritual dimension" (39). Willard also cites the Grimm fairy tale, "Godfather Death," as an influence; and the ball game wager made by her personification of Death recalls Applegate's deal with Joe Boyd in *The Year the Yankees Lost the Pennant* and points to Gideon Clarke's high-stakes contest in *The Iowa Baseball Confederacy*. As magical realism,[3] *Things* also bears similarities to *Spitballs and Holy Water*, *The Seventh Babe*, and *Shoeless Joe*, which predate it by seven, five, and two years respectively; and in its intense depiction of a spiritualist folk healer, it prepares the way for *Havana Heat* sixteen years later. The novel's uniqueness, however, lies in its extensive array of spiritual phenomena that, more than in any other baseball novel, swirl around the characters and endow their otherwise unremarkable existence with a shimmering otherworldliness. The book's dreams, visions,

---

[3] Elsewhere in her writings, the author acknowledges the great Colombian writer, Gabriel García Márquez, whom we discussed in chapter 3 as a prime influence on Jerome Charyn. The key to convincing readers, says García Márquez, is to depict the supernatural and fantastic with detailed descriptions and complete naturalness, writing with the same expression—"a brick face"—that a venerable storyteller would present to grandchildren (*Telling Time*, 31, 35).

out-of-body experiences, shifts in time, and heavenly ball games not only make for delightful reading, but also assert that life is lived on many planes and must be affirmed in all its manifestations.

The Earthly Framework

The earthly plot of the novel takes place just before and after America's entry into World War II, 1941-1942 to be exact, primarily in Ann Arbor, Michigan. The story depicts the lives of two families, the Bishops and Harkissians, focusing on the love relationship of Clare Bishop and Ben Harkissian, and the parallel but different lives of Ben and his twin brother, Willie. The two families are fatefully linked when seventeen-year-old Ben aims a baseball into the darkness at a white bird[4], instead striking and paralyzing the teenage Clare, who is strolling in the distance. In her invalid state, Clare is visited by a spirit guide called the Ancestress and by a repentant Ben, with whom she falls in love before he must leave for the war. Later she is healed with the help of a black spiritualist named Cold Friday, and participates in a fanciful showdown ball game between dead Major Leaguers and the families of Ben and his friends, who are scattered throughout the world in military service. If the locals win, the young men buy time and survive the war.

---

[4] In *The Natural*, birds are a key image, and the baseball is identified as a white dove. Here, in a book filled with bird imagery, Ben aims his hit *at* a white dove and strikes a girl instead. In W. P. Kinsella's second novel, *The Iowa Baseball Confederacy*, two years after *Things*, we again see the ball-dove identification.

Spiritual Links to Space-Time

A. The Heavenly Dimension

The "real-time" action in space-time is penetrated five times by divine intervention, whimsically depicted as the throw of a baseball from God's hand. The first instance is in the book's opening paragraph, cited above, which warrants further attention. There the "River of Time," along which God and the angels play, is precisely what separates the Creator from his creation, eternity from space-time. Movement over this boundary creates tension throughout the novel. The next lines read: "Hundreds of spheres rest like white stones on the bottom of the river5 and hundreds rise like bubbles from the water and fly to His hand that alone brings things to pass and gives them their true colors. What a show!" (3). The word "alone" establishes God as the final reference point for Willard; the many and varied spiritual wonders she will depict, unorthodox though they are, stem ultimately not from her characters (as they admit), but from God.

Then comes the pitch that crosses the River of Time[6] and enters human space, setting the story in motion: "He tosses a white ball which breaks into a yellow ball which breaks into a red ball, and in the northeast corner of the Sahara Desert the sand shifts and buries eight camels. The two herdsmen escape, and in a small town in southern Michigan Wanda Harkissian goes into labor with twins. She will name them Ben and Willie, but it's Esau and Jacob all over again" (3).

---

[5] White stones as almost magical building blocks of creation are found in García Márquez. They recur in *Things*, when the near-death experience of Clare's mother, Helen Bishop, is recounted (15).

[6] Just as baseball links God and man, so it connects people to each other. The Harkissians and Bishops only meet because of the ball with which Ben wounds Clare. Significantly, it too went over a river, at Ann Arbor's Island Park.

By introducing the rival twin sons of Isaac, Willard establishes another biblical context. Just as Jacob deviously acquired his brother's birthright and their father's blessing (Genesis 25 & 27), so Willie, in another sparkling early paragraph, makes a deal in utero[7] (!) that seals their fate: "In the damp night of the womb, when millions of chromosomes are gearing up for the game of life, the soul of Willie says to the soul of Ben, 'Listen, you can be firstborn and get out of this cave first if you'll give me everything else. Brains, charm, and good looks'" (3). The great difference between the brothers determines their fate throughout the story and, it is hinted, in eternity.

The final sentence of the book's first page, which functions like a literary prologue or a musical upbeat, notes the details of the bargain. Whereas Willie would be left-brained, right-handed, mathematically inclined, and rich, Ben would receive "the sinister mysteries of the left hand and the dark meadows of the right hemisphere, where clocks lose their numbers and all roads lead to everywhere" (3-4). These last words establish from the outset the relative nature of space-time in the novel[8], which makes possible the spiritual shenanigans that follow.

The other four divine pitches have these words in common: "In Paradise, the Lord of the Universe tosses" (36, 147, 218, 263). Each time, the playful action in heaven prompts something on earth, often in two places half a world apart, and each time there is a variation in the ball's break from one color to another. The final color of the pitches is, respectively, red, gold, green, black, and gold. One could speculate on some equivalency between

---

[7] W. P. Kinsella's short story "The Battery," which appeared the same year as *Things*, shows twin boys playing catch in their mother's womb.

[8] Several other examples of this follow, such as in the description of Helen Bishop's gift of second sight patterned after Willard's aunt and given in chapter 2: "The long tunnel of time leading from her past to her future closed down. Time became space, a great pathless field" (15).

the color and the occasion;[9] more likely, however, the changing hues are simply intended to be a dazzling attribute of God's creation, whose hand "alone," writes Willard, "brings things to pass and gives them their true colors" (3).

The Lord says nothing in any of these brief interludes, but he is quoted five times elsewhere, first in a conversation with the archangel Gabriel, then twice in brief responses to something said on earth, comments that are not heard by the people. The fourth remark, challenging Ben's notion that his Pacific island was hardly worth God's time to make it, parodies the Lord's rebuke in the biblical book of Job. For instance, instead of "Where were you when I laid the earth's foundation?" (38:4), God asks Ben, "*Where were you when I made this island?*" (174-75). His final comment, also heard only by the reader, comes just before the life-and-death ball game, and is reassuring: "*The very hairs of your head are numbered*" (253), a New Testament witness to God's concern for his children.

Whenever God speaks, the words are written in italics,[10] as are other remarks made from outside of space-time, such as ancestors beckoning to Clare's Aunt Helen in a near-death experience, "*Come over*" (16), imagined words of advice from Ben's dead father (20), a macabre conversation between Death and Nazi air marshal, Hermann Goering, and Hal's voice from the airplane (262).

---

[9] One could speculate that red signifies Esau, as the Bible describes him, with his red skin and red stew; gold might represent life, as in the life-giving home run; black corresponds to the child's death in Burma and the threat of the ballplayers' demise should they lose. Green is the final color in the only sequence (147) that has two, not three, colors. I see nothing in that quirky scene to warrant equating it with the motif of life, growth, or unripeness normally associated with green. Green is the second color in the sequence that ends with black.

[10] The use of italics to indicate a distinctive narrative level is also an important feature of *The Iowa Baseball Confederacy* and *Havana Heat.*

B. The Ancestress

The most prominent non-biblical spirit being in *Things* is an old woman called the Ancestress, a figure inspired by the near-death experience of the author's aunt, who was invited, but declined, to cross a river to reach her deceased ancestors. "What if," Willard wondered, "one of those ancestors crossed the river and joined the living.... The character of the Ancestress in my novel is one answer to that question" (*Telling Time*, 36).

The Ancestress enters space-time seven times to serve as a guardian spirit to Clare and later to Ben. She appears in various forms—as an old woman visible only to a few select people, as an animal or insect (a bird, a fly), and even as an inanimate object (a knife). In chapter 2, on her first visit to Clare in the hospital after the accident, she leads the girl out of her body to tutor her, and thus the reader, in the phenomenon of spirit travel that is the premise of the novel. She explains that she has been with Clare since birth and with her mother before that. The Ancestress introduces the prominent image of human beings as houses (or "*bone-house*[s]" [75]). When lamps are burning within, they are alive; when the house is dark, abandoned, they have given up the ghost. While this is initially a source of wonder to Clare, it also prepares her for her life-saving mission later when Ben is on the verge of death.

The third appearance of the Ancestress is a significant one. It illustrates how she enters space-time and Clare moves in and out of her body. As the convent bells chime, Clare "listened for the faint final stroke and heard a ping of glass shattered far away. The thirteenth stroke. The Ancestress hovered at the foot of the bed" (74). By now, Clare is practiced at her transition, slipping "like fog out of her flesh" (74).[11]

---

[11] These two descriptions of ghostly transition are similar to the magic described by W. P. Kinsella, whose characters slip backward and forward through "cracks in time."

On this trip, the Ancestress lets Clare be her own guide, following her own impulses. These impulses take her to Hermann Goering's lavish hunting lodge, where she witnesses the Nazi leader's conversation with a gentleman in black, whom he addresses as Herr Death. This brief segment provides links to several themes in the novel, including the Bishops' ancestor who painted the kaiser, the Harkissians' talisman coin, and the relationship of Death to those who serve him.

The Ancestress's last four appearances, which will be discussed in the following sections, are in support of Clare's desire to aid Ben as he faces death, first in the Pacific theater, then in the hospital at home, and finally in the life-and-death ball game. There, as in her earlier visits to space-time, the wise figure from outside of space-time brings an eternal perspective to life that helps the living enjoy and appreciate it more.

C. Herr Death and Mr. Knochen

The antithesis of Nancy Willard's Ancestress, who enters space-time from beyond the grave to nurture life, is the aptly named Mr. Knochen (=*bones*, German), also called "Death" and, by Goering, "Herr Death."[12] Unlike the Ancestress, who is known only to those with the gift of second sight, Knochen is seen (dare one say it?) in the flesh as an itinerant spiritualist who conducts séances in private homes. Commended by friends to the Bishops, he cuts an otherworldly figure upon arriving at their home: "Pale, thin face and white hair combed straight back…. He peeled off his gloves, black leather,…exposing the pale meat below" (106). Clare is alarmed at the sight, which reminds her of the black-gloved coroner at a drowning she saw placing two silver coins

---

[12] Knochen/Death bears some resemblance to the Grimms' Godfather Death figure, who granted great powers to his godson physician, then took the young man's life when he twice deceived the godfather.

on the eyes of a dead boy. She then recognizes him as Herr Death, whom she saw with Goering, and wonders if he has come for her.

Ostensibly, Knochen is there to facilitate communication with the dead, and indeed the spirit of Helen's deceased baby sings a lullaby through the open mouth of the sleeping Clare. But the visit, it turns out, has two greater purposes. When Knochen says he is looking for a match to his silver coin, Ben, who keeps the talisman on a string around his neck, is alerted to the fact that he must soon face Death. When Knochen uses a Ouija board to record spirit messages, it taps out the name of Cold Friday, the local spiritualist who eventually will bring about Clare's healing. Though Knochen has met them in space-time, the séance moves the participants to the edge of it to seek knowledge from beyond the River of Time. "Ben found that every part of him was shaking except his hands, which felt as if they were in another corner of the universe, dabbling and dipping themselves in the streams of no-time" (112).

Death next appears rowing a lifeboat in the Pacific Ocean, where Ben and his commanding officer, Captain Cooper, have been floating for days in a raft after their little island was inundated. Ben and Cooper have only survived because of the intervention of Clare and the Ancestress, who have sent them food in the form of a small shark.[13] The raft sequences are dreamlike; they are on the edge of space-time. As at the séance, where one could no longer hear the clock, "time stopped on the high seas" (192). Death ushers Cooper into the next world, placing a silver coin on his left eye and asking Ben for the match, the talisman coin. Though Death beckons Ben too, the lucky coin gives him a reprieve, which he uses to challenge Death to a bet, a game of baseball. Reminiscent of Goethe's Mephistopheles

---

[13] Willard based chapter 25, called "Birdlight," on a *LIFE* magazine report of three sailors' thirty-four-day lifeboat ordeal in 1942.

and Wallop's Applegate, Death writes a contract "on the air with one pale finger, which trailed a thin line of smoke" (195). The stakes: a new lease on life beyond the war, or immediate death for Ben and his Ann Arbor team-mates, the South Avenue Rovers.

Death's final appearance—divided into three parts by cutaways to Ben in the hospital and Hal flying home—is as coach of the Dead Knights, a ghostly team of long-dead major league stars like the famous cornfield players in *Shoeless Joe*: "They did not run onto the field. They simply appeared, as if they had broken through a wall of air, or an invisible ray into visibility" (254). To increase his chances of winning, Death had arranged for the Rovers' team bus to crash, forcing the players' mothers to perform in their stead. After miraculous healings, Clare and Ben join the team, as does twin brother Willie. But Willie is seduced and blackmailed by Death, who aims to recruit a Judas. "I want you to keep my records, plead my cause. Snuff out hope[14] wherever you find it" (260). Willie's first reaction is to decline, but when Death tells him that his dishonest dealings will lead to a trial and offers him "every living thing in the world,"[15] he accepts. As a token of their partnership, the magic coin is given to Willie. We can only speculate on his fate, recalling the conversation with Goering, who went in league with Death for greed's sake. The final lines of the Goering talk bodes ill for Willie: "*What power did you think I would give you in exchange? The power to meet your own death? Don't you know that to those who serve me the power is already given*" (76). Goering later met his own death by committing suicide. Perhaps Willie may do the same.

---

[14] At the séance, Knochen misquotes the famous love chapter, 1 Corinthians 13, stating that hope, not love, was the greatest virtue. It may be that he is trying to deceive his biblically illiterate listeners and steer them away from love. It is also possible that, like the Devil, he doesn't comprehend love and can't combat it. Thus, in seeking to undermine human life, he directs his new underling to attack hope.

[15] This echoes the temptation of Christ, who of course rejected the Devil's offers.

D. Cold Friday: The Root Doctor and Mysterious Healer

The most colorful character of *Things Invisible to See* makes only one appearance, but it seems like more. The buildup to the spiritualist healer known as Cold Friday is a perfect example of Willard's narrative principle of releasing information gradually. "The journalist tries to give you the facts," she writes. "The narrative writer tries not to. Part of telling a story well is keeping information back and letting it escape when the time is right" (*Telling Time*, 63). Many interesting events or images may not be understood until a subsequent reading, which then delights us as the hidden layers of meaning emerge. Other images may register only faintly with the reader, but subconsciously they may register enough to enhance the crucial information "when the time is right."

When at the onset of the séance Clare peers into the fireplace, she sees an image of Death wrestling with a tall, distinctively dressed woman. This turns out to be her healer, but there is no hint of that at first. Then the Ouija pointer spells out this message, letter by letter, as named by Knochen: "C-O-L-D F-R-I-D-A-Y D-O-N-E D-I-E-D F-I-V-E T-I-M-E-S" (113). The message is so mysterious that Helen believes it to be a hoax, and though a street name is added, the subject is dropped, unresolved.

Cold Friday is next mentioned in a letter to Ernestina, a local black cleaning lady whose son, Stilts, played ball with Ben Harkissian. The reader, but not those at the séance, now understands that Cold Friday is a person, not a day of the week. Only much later, when Ernestina is enlisted to baby-sit Davy, the Bishops' young son, does the reader receive more information about the mercurial healer. Ernestina regales Davy with tales of ghosts, superstitions, and folk healings done by a "root doctor" (208)[16] and

---

[16] This folk figure, who may deal in magical or medicinal roots and keep them in bottles, is prominent in *The Seventh Babe*.

goes on to explain the origin of the healer's name and her ability to overcome death. As a young girl, she survived a legendary Friday cold wave when others froze and died. Then she revived after four other deadly incidents, becoming a local legend and establishing a healing practice in Ann Arbor.

When Davy, misunderstanding, speaks of a "rude doctor on Catherine Street" (230) and volunteers other details that confirm the Ouija information, Ben makes the connection to someone who can heal Clare and runs rejoicing from the room. As he does so, the narrator launches into an extravagant three-page (231-33) mix of magical realism and tall tale that contains far too many images and motifs to explicate, but we can highlight a few details on the nature of Cold Friday's mysterious person and healing practice. We learn that she has African facial features and is believed to speak the Gullah or Trinidad language, dialects connected to an African folk religion that came to the Americas through the slave trade.[17] The fetish of placing clippings of her nails or hair around the neighborhood "gives her power over the people who live there. It also gives them protection from devils, perturbed spirits, and the evil eye" (231).

Her power sets Cold Friday apart from her mortal neighbors, who are reluctant to call her anything but the root doctor. Though physically present in 1942's Michigan, she, like others in this novel, moves in the ghostly realm beyond space-time. "She was born the year the stars fell" (213),[18] reports Ernestina, and no record exists of her name or age. Her healing powers come from God, who also granted her "a pass, signed with her

---

[17] Cf. the later chapter on *Havana Heat* for information about another blend of African religion with Christianity, called *santería*.

[18] If this is a reference to Satan's pre-Eden fall from heaven, when a third of the stars and heavenly beings fell with him, it attributes an ageless, ancient quality to Cold Friday. However, Willard adds that Davy wasn't sure if that quote referred to her or to the owl he thought he heard.

name, good for traveling between the lands of the living and the dead" (233). This reconfirms Nancy Willard's cosmology of the biblical creator God, who willingly allows other forms of spiritual communication than those found in orthodox Judeo-Christian writings.

When at last Cold Friday appears, in the book's penultimate chapter 33, the elaborate description of the healer's appearance confirms Clare's vision of her at the séance, wrestling with Death. There are more references to silver as a magical medium and an antidote to the Devil, and indeed, the diagnosis of Clare's paralysis, beyond the baseball concussion, comes through a silver coin. "Like a priest giving communion, she put the quarter on Clare's tongue.... Clare spit out the quarter. But how changed! It was now as black as the hand that received it, a bright moon eclipsed" (245). The root doctor declares that Clare has been conjured and sets out to determine the source of the spell. Using chicken blood that magically courses along an anatomical chart and returns to its bottle, she identifies the curse as an ancient one, originating with Satan's fall from heaven, moving through the primeval waters, entering the body of Eve, and corrupting the fraternal relationship of her sons. "And Cain [read: Willie] said to his brother, 'You be firstborn and give me the brains. You kin have everything else.' And that spell got itself handed down, hand over hand, 'cause that spell is so evil. The hand that worked the spell on you didn't make it. And now we's got to take that spell off" (246).

Cold Friday looses several birds (favorite spiritual equivalents for Willard) with the strong plea for God to heal Clare and take the demon from her. She spreads hot coals on the floor, sings Clare to sleep, and slips away. In the following passage, with hints of biblical overtones, God defeats a demon, Clare is healed, and life is affirmed: "And because the bureau had now caught fire and the edge of the bedspread crackled into flames, and because the demon had met his match and the deep sleep of Clare's bones was ended, and because Clare herself wanted to live and wanted Ben to live also, she staggered out of bed and ran into the hall…. 'Look!' screamed Davy. 'Clare's *running!*'" (247).

Cold Friday, feared dead in the flames, has gone, and with her the family silver and other treasures as her fee. It was as if she had never been there, and the fire from her magic coals had created no damage.

The Cosmic Showdown: Life and Love vs. Death and Deceit

In a tour de force of a finale, replete with miracles and spiritual wonders, chapter 34 nimbly moves between three strands of plot to resolve the pending tensions of the novel. In the first strand, the Ben-Willie relationship that began the novel gives way to the Ben-Clare plot as the central story line. (Willie, as we saw above, has made another deal, trading his family allegiance for Death's employ.) Because Cold Friday defeated the demon of paralysis in the purifying fire of chapter 33, Clare is now free to help Ben, who after the bus accident lies near death, his lamps almost extinguished. The Ancestress suggests that Ben's love for Clare is what will revive him, and she takes Clare to the hospital to breathe on the lamps and re-light them. His recovery is the second miracle, after Clare's healing.

Another strand of the denouement is Hal Bishop's return flight from Los Alamos to Ann Arbor. The small plane with the mysterious cargo (probably connected with top-secret atomic research) runs out of fuel but continues to fly in silence. The pilot and co-pilot grasp for explanations. "Only Hal believed his eyes. The engines were silent. But under the wing he saw the ghostly shapes of children, animals, birds, bearing them up" (261). Again, deliverance comes through ancestors, in various forms, from beyond space-time. In his joy, Hal sings the classic hymn "Amazing Grace" so fervently that his wife, Helen, can hear it far away and thinks it might be Grandpa, the most devout believer in the family. In response to her wondering what it all means, Father Legg's answer, "It's a miracle" (262), is twice more correct. Earlier he had hailed as miraculous the healing of Clare and Ben; now he refers to Hal's rescue and to Helen's hearing his voice. The well-known words that Hal sings, "*When we've been there ten thousand years/Bright shining as the sun*," suggest the ghostly shapes that lifted up his plane. They also link traditional Christianity with the ancestral visits that course through the novel.

The third story strand of chapter 34 is Ben's baseball wager with Death for the lives of the South Avenue Rovers. The high-stakes game, brief though it is, is a wonder of magical realism, blending living people in space-time with "translucent" ballplayers with a crowd of ancestor spectators, "a vast, silent throng that receded as if on invisible waves, the women in white, the men in black, the lovely fabric of their presence growing faint among the far-off dead, turning in those farthest from her to feathers, wings, the faces of birds" (260). Still, we wonder, how will the Rovers' mothers (plus Clare, healed and in-body, and Willie) defeat the Hall-of-Famers?

One answer comes from Death, who admits that his players want the living to win. With all life's pain and trouble, they would gladly choose it again, and they want to help the Rovers keep it. Another answer comes from the Ancestress, who appears in the form of a buzzing fly to bring advice for Clare, the Rovers' pitcher. Like Sister Timothy in *Spitballs and Holy Water*, Clare can use magic to defeat Major Leaguers. Though she cannot persuade her guardian spirit to "go into the ball" (258), she can "*Put some stuff on it.... The stuff of being alive. Morning, evening, the first snow, the last snow, bells, daisies, hubcaps, silver dollars, ice cream, hummingbirds, love.... You say it very softly over the ball before you throw it*" (258).

His lamps now ablaze, Ben bolts the hospital and speeds to the ballpark, where he comes to the plate as the tying run. (That a book should end with a tie score is unexpected, even if we can presume that the Rovers will go on to win. Perhaps that is to be consistent with the premise that they are only buying time, not ultimately defeating Death.) The final, lyrical paragraph completes the denouement of the three strands of the plot, linked by baseball to God in heaven:

> In Paradise, the Lord of the Universe tosses a green ball which breaks into a silver ball which breaks into a gold ball, and a small plane lands safely at Willow Run and Hal Bishop climbs out, singing for joy. He is too far away to hear the crack of the bat, like a tree falling all alone in the forest. But he hears the distant cheering. Clare starts running and Ben runs after her as they round the bases, past the living and the dead, heading at top speed for home (263).

Thus concludes a sumptuous tale of life and death, entwined by the mysterious spiritual offshoots of heaven that make their way into space-time. Nancy Willard has taken us through a poetic spiritual battle, where, as in several other baseball novels, the power of love and life ultimately prevails.

Appendix to Chapter 6

Spiritual and Narrative Dimensions in *Things Invisible to See*

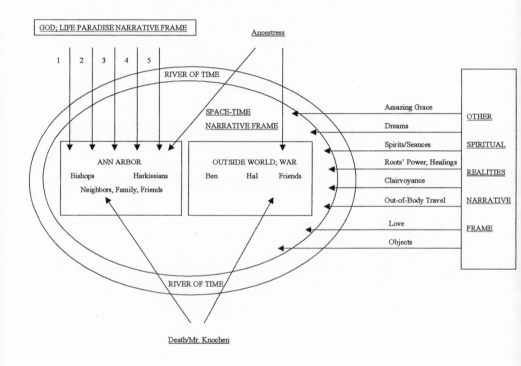

Inning 7:

An American Apocalypse: Religious Parody in *The Iowa Baseball Confederacy*

Just as with his first novel, *Shoeless Joe*, W. P. Kinsella has concocted in *The Iowa Baseball Confederacy* a rich mixture of local color, magic, baseball, love, and religion. Both novels use the national pastime to laud the power of human imagination and take the reader on fanciful trips through time and space—*Shoeless Joe* with a smooth, subtle tale of familial love, *The IBC* with an intense, apocalyptic adventure of passion and death. To gain access to the secrets of Kinsella's apocalypse, the reader, as in *Things Invisible to See* and other works of magical realism, must be willing to suspend disbelief and trust that magic is possible in this life, that the immutable forces of time and death can be defeated. If not, he will not accept the outlandish premise of the novel: A man named Gideon Clarke attempts to prove the validity of an obsession inherited from his father, Matthew, namely that the

1908 Chicago Cubs, contrary to all surviving records, really did play a fantastic forty-day exhibition game against a collection of Iowa All-Stars.[1] Seventy years after the fact, Gideon sneaks through a "crack in time" (7) to relive the epic struggle that took place in the tiny town of Big Inning on the outskirts of Iowa City. Once in Big Inning, Gideon encounters a cultural and religious maelstrom of obsession and intolerance, which swirls figuratively around the rainy ball game as a literal flood begins to rise. The deluge, which recreates the punishing flood of Noah, destroys the fanaticism both of the players and of the spectators, and hope is offered only to those who develop a sense of tolerance and self-sacrifice. Upon examining the passions and beliefs that surround the game, one finds that Kinsella has given us less a baseball story than an elaborate religious parody. He has created an American apocalypse.

There are three religious systems at work in Big Inning, Iowa (outlined in a chart at the end of this chapter), a fanciful trinity: fundamentalist Christianity, caricatured in the bizarre sect known as the "Twelve-Hour Church of Time Immemorial"; the American Indian religion of a Sac-Fox warrior named Drifting Away and the gods he calls "grandfathers"; and the game of baseball, specifically the marathon struggle between the Cubs and the Iowa Baseball Confederacy. Each religion has its own set of principles and powers—though baseball borrows images and tenets from the other two belief systems—and none emerges as all-powerful. Rather, Kinsella uses expressions such as "something happened" and "the powers that be" to indicate that an undefined and punishing but vaguely benevolent force is in

---

[1] Philip Roth has a similar bizarre event in *The Great American Novel*, where a ninety-year-old former sportswriter tries to convince the public that a third major league, the Patriot League, once existed but was purged from baseball's historical records.

final control of man's destiny.[2] Johnny Baron, the lone Confederacy survivor in 1978, calls it "Whatever power there is that lurks around and evens things out" (119). Thus, as the local belief systems in Big Inning become more polarized, something intervenes to restore balance to the universe. Johnny Baron continues, "Well now, there was this game, and things got a little out of hand. The powers that be straightened things out. They erased the Confederacy" (120). How then did things get out of hand, and why was it necessary to erase the Confederacy? The answer for Kinsella lies in the obsessions of all humans and their religions.

The Religion of Baseball

As noted in the introduction above, the obsession of people like Matthew Clarke and his son, Gideon, can be termed "religious," conforming as it does to Frederick Streng's theological definition of "an ultimate frame of reference [that] claims the power and insight to distinguish what is real or true from what is secondary, derivative, or even false" (6). Matthew knew that the IBC "was going to become the most important element in his life" (27); he and Gideon are both convinced of the truth of their revealed insight into the IBC and devote their lives to acting on the revelation.

In addition to the internal religious attributes of the Clarkes' baseball quest, Kinsella also describes the sport in external religious terms, such as outlined by Joe Price in my introduction, which create a belief system comparable to any other (5). Kinsella attributes divine qualities to baseball

---

[2] Because of the lessons and hope provided at the end of the novel, it is possible to suggest that the power behind the apocalypse is "benevolent." This is not to overlook the presence of evil in *The IBC* (25), the "evil sense of humor" in the world power (102), or the "cold, evil white" lightning-bearing clouds (237) over the game.

through Matthew Clarke, for whom his first game was something of an epiphany: "It was just like I'd discovered the meaning of the universe" (43). Baseball also displays for Matthew the perfection and infinity associated with the nature of God and with Streng's "ultimate dimension":

> Name me a more perfect game! Name me a game with more possibilities for magic, wizardry, voodoo, hoodoo, enchantment, obsession, possession…. No mere mortal could have dreamed up the dimensions of a baseball field. No man could be that perfect. Abner Doubleday, if he did indeed invent the game, must have received divine guidance. And the field runs to infinity…. The foul lines run on forever, forever diverging…. Hell, there's no place in the *world* that's not part of a baseball field (44-45).

Echoing themes we saw in *Shoeless Joe*, both Gideon Clarke and his father see themselves as "prophets" (25, 29), while Matthew also refers to himself as "one of the chosen" (45). Gideon, so named because his father, like the biblical Gideon, played the trumpet, calls himself a "one-man religion" (112). Each is described as an "evangelist" (45, 96). After being struck by lightning, Matthew Clarke, a modern-day Moses with the name of the first evangelist, received the history of the IBC "carved on stone tablets in his memory" (29).

On the one hand, prophets are blessed with special knowledge, and "wise men lay up knowledge" (Prov 10:14), but on the other they accept that they "are meant to be derided and maligned" (25). Initially, Matthew Clarke accepts the two-edged nature of his calling. "I'm glad it happened to me," he says. "It ain't easy, but you should be so lucky" (45). Later, however, after years of ridicule and fruitless search for confirmation of the IBC,

Matthew Clarke wearies of the quest. He commits suicide at a major league game by tilting his head into a line drive, thereby passing to his son the prophetic mantle and—note the biblical use of "visit"—its curse. "I was overflowing with knowledge, and boiling with righteous indignation because not a soul in the world cared about what I knew. Whatever had been visited upon my father was now transplanted into my brain like a pacemaker installed next to a fluttering heart" (50).

The knowledge of the IBC, like the calling of a prophet, has its dark side as well. Despite efforts of the powers that be to erase the Confederacy, "Bits and pieces have survived, like rumors, like buried evil unearthed and activated" (25). It is the power of this "evil" to arouse human compulsion, feed man's obsessions, and eventually destroy him. "His knowledge of the Confederacy destroyed his life, and some say my knowledge of the Confederacy is destroying mine" (25). Even as the apocalypse descends on Big Inning, Gideon insists, "I've got to know what happens" (233) and "above everything else I've got to find out how the game comes out and why" (252). Like Goethe's Faust, Gideon pursues his obsession for knowledge even though it costs the lives of others, and as a prophet and a wealthy man, he also experiences the woeful insight of King Solomon: "For in much wisdom is much grief; and he that increaseth knowledge increaseth sorrow" (Eccl 1:18).[3] Gideon has another obsession that also has a great bearing on

---

[3] Along with the book of Revelation, the fall of man at the tree of the knowledge of good and evil, the flood, the story of Gideon in the book of Judges, and the Psalms, the book of Ecclesiastes seems to have the most biblical bearing on Kinsella's novel. One summary calls Ecclesiastes "a protest against the ever-present temptation of faith to shore up its own uncertainty with dogmatism and against the constant tendency of human understanding to overrate its potentiality" (Guthrie 320). This holds true when we consider the dogmatic and obsessive collision of the three religions, which led to the apocalyptic ballgame.

the story. He desires to possess two women: Sunny, his mercurial, wandering wife in 1978, and Sarah, his forbidden love of 1908.

There are other, lesser comparisons of baseball with religion, and they are based on the smug intransigence of the wicked described in Psalm 10:6: "He hath said in his heart, I shall not be moved: for I shall never be in adversity." Cub shortstop Joe Tinker, when asked what it's like to be in the big leagues, responds, "For baseball players it's as close to heaven as any of us will ever get...you set your eye on the top and never stop until you get there, and never let them move you after you do" (228-29). Likewise, Gideon's friend and fellow time traveler, Stan, is said to be in a "state of rapture" (252) as he achieves his dream of playing successfully against Major Leaguers. Another parody of rapture, or a kind of ascension, is in the death by lightning of the Confederacy right fielder. Molten tines of lightning cross beneath his corpse and bear it majestically to the sky.[4]

When the Iowa City statue called the Black Angel begins to make its way from the cemetery toward the ball field, the efforts of a priest (reading from Ecclesiastes) are not sufficient to hold it back: "the Angel would not be moved" (255). In a play on words that fits the mood of the game, fans debating the merits of their favorite players remain "unmoved" (262) by the others' arguments.

"But the Confederacy hangs in tenaciously. Like everyone else in and around Big Inning, they will not be moved" (270). The appropriately named Confederacy player Bill Stiff refuses to acknowledge that a mammoth home run cannot be tracked down. He pursues it toward the horizon,

---

[4] A similar parody of religious rapture, a calling away to heaven, is found in Kinsella's first novel, *Shoeless Joe*. This work, which also portrays baseball as an object of religious devotion and its true fans as a chosen people, concludes with a chapter titled "The Rapture of J. D. Salinger." Moving through the centerfield gate with the ghostly players of the past, the reclusive author enters the spiritual realm they inhabit between games.

leaps "into infinity" (263), and disappears. Days later he is reported racing through New Mexico, still straining for the imaginary ball. A deceased teammate continues his obsession in death, as the embarrassed pallbearers cannot remove his coffin: "Bad News Galloway, it seems, will not be moved" (267). The Cubs are no less determined. Their injured third baseman continues play while lying on a cot. The manager "wanted to take him out of the game entirely, but Steinfeldt, like everyone else in Big Inning, will not be moved" (283).

The Twelve-Hour Church

Another element of the religious parody in *The Iowa Baseball Confederacy* is the strange group that calls itself the Twelve-Hour Church of Time Immemorial, so named because its members live on a schedule twelve hours removed from the rest of the society. They sleep during the day and plow the fields by miners' lamps at night. The sect has a favorite hymn, a theme song for the church, indeed for the town of Big Inning, and it reinforces a main theme of the novel: "The Church of God is marching, / I shall not be moved" (189).

The idea of remaining unmoved connotes the virtues of steadfastness and loyalty to God in the face of worldly temptations (cf. Ps 21:7), but it can also refer to the wicked, as cited above in Psalm 10:6: "He hath said in his heart, I shall not be moved: for I shall never be in adversity." This applies to the self-satisfied zealots of the Twelve-Hour Church, whose attitude can at best be called Iowa "stubbornness" (306), at worst obsession and fanaticism. It seems that they are living on Indian land but refuse to leave because of a storied event that happened to their pastor. "Elder Womple was out walking one afternoon, reading his Bible, when the book was plucked from his hands by an unseen source. Slammed the book on the ground, it did, and the book was petrified and rooted to the earth when Elder Womple tried to pick it up" (190).[5] Taking this as a sign from God, despite government objections, the sect built its church on this spot and refused to budge.

In the first days of the ball game, Elder Womple senses the magical atmosphere and attributes it to God's presence: "The very air is charged with the Spirit" (204). He does not, however, acknowledge that another spirit might be at work and that he is more an object of its wrath than a beloved prophet. At the height of the flood, when warned that the church should be abandoned, the pastor insists, "We are not so easily moved" (283). The price of his obsession is the physical destruction of both Womple and the church building in the flood and the disappearance of the Twelve-Hour sect.

The Grandfathers

The third aspect of Kinsella's apocalyptic parody is the folk religion of the American Indians, which has points in common with both the baseball and the Christian belief systems. In addition to his own lively imagination, the author's prime source for this part of the novel is *Black Elk Speaks*, the life story of an Oglala Sioux warrior and medicine man and a book that has been called a "North American Bible of all tribes."[6] Just as Kinsella has

---

[5] The story goes on to explain that "Of course, the Good Book was frozen open to the story of Gideon" (190), the Old Testament figure in the book of Judges. The biblical Gideon was the leader of a small group of Israelites who claimed land from superior numbers of other tribes. By blowing trumpets, breaking pitchers, and carrying lamps (cf. miners' lamps!), they gave the impression of a much larger force and prevailed. Their rallying cry was "The sword of the Lord, and of Gideon," which became the title of another favorite hymn of the Big Inning church (190). The coincidence of Gideon Clarke's name and his trumpet cause the church members to wonder if he is perhaps a prophet, not only of the IBC but also of the Twelve-Hour Church.

[6] Vine Deloria, "Introduction," in Neihardt, xi.

adapted concepts and passages from the Bible for *The Iowa Baseball Confederacy*, so his text reflects the words of Black Elk.

The supreme being in *Black Elk Speaks* is not so clearly defined as is Jehovah of the Bible. Black Elk uses several terms, including the singular forms of address "Spirit of the World" and "Great Spirit" and the plural forms "Powers of the World" and "The Powers." In a somewhat more personal form of address, the Great Spirit is called "Grandfather" and the Powers are referred to as "Grandfathers" and numbered as six: powers of the West, the North, the East, the South, the Sky, and the Earth (25). Still, says Black Elk, "the Powers of the Universe…are One Power" (238).

The Indian gods in *The IBC* are indeed called "the grandfathers," though limited by Kinsella to four in number, and we learn that it is they who have arranged the game. The equivalent of their prophet is Drifting Away, a gallant warrior possessed of many divine attributes. People who "believe in" Drifting Away can see him; he can change the course of the river and alter reality to keep the underdog Confederacy in the game. "Yes," he states, "I tamper with the reality of Johnson County, Iowa…. I *am* the reality of Johnson County. I can take life or I can give it" (177).[7]

Drifting Away is "always as close as your shadow" (246), yet "no one wakes unless I wish them to" (206). He transcends both time and space, moving between generations and loping with giant strides across and through the countryside. In seeking to restore the scattered soul of his dead wife, Onamata, Drifting Away becomes an agent of rebirth and renewal, and by rescuing Gideon from imminent death in the flood, he is also a "sav-

---

[7] There is a parallel here to Black Elk, who as warrior/medicine man could take life or give it. At one point, he calls himself a "Wanekia," the name given to Wovoka, an Indian "Messiah" and leader of the 1889-1890 Ghost Dance religion. The title "Wanekia" translates as "One Who Makes Live," a savior (233, 269).

ior." In so doing, the Indian "sacrifices" his extraordinary powers, and like Christ he becomes mortal to save others. The metamorphosis of Drifting Away—"he shrinks before my eyes until he is the size of an ordinary mortal" (270)—parallels that of Doc Graham in *Shoeless Joe*. The aspiring young ballplayer named Archie Graham sacrifices his quest for a major league career when he saves the narrator's choking daughter, and he is visibly transformed into the old country doctor.

Drifting Away, like Gideon, is a "chosen" one (180), but he is also a murderer, a fanatic, and a penitent. Although Kinsella's sympathies unquestionably lie with the Indian culture, the author does not create a flawless protagonist. Drifting Away did kill innocent campers and threaten to kill again. He is just as adamant as the white settlers about not being moved from his land, and the same Psalm 10 that quoted the wicked as saying, "I shall not be moved," could be applied to Drifting Away's unseen activity: "He sitteth in the lurking places of the villages: in the secret places doth he murder the innocent" (10:8).

Drifting Away also won't be moved from the desire to repossess his wife, though less out of pride than of anguish. The murder of Onamata by the settlers occurred, he believes, because of his own weakness. "I could have saved Onamata. She was my life. I have been doing what the people of the strange church over there would call penance. The grandfathers are giving me a final chance" (246). The chance consists of helping the underdog Confederacy to defeat the mighty Cubs, the equivalent of the Indians beating the cavalry; but in struggling against the Cubs, he is also confronting the grandfathers. Drifting Away's relationship to them is much like Jacob's wrestling with the angel, and the ball game has been established by the grandfathers as a test of his mettle. They agree to return his wife to him if the Confederacy wins.

The connection to baseball goes beyond this test. The game is also part of his religion and a bridge to the otherwise alien white culture: "Baseball is the one single thing the white man has done right" (177). Earlier in the novel, he had described the conflict between white and Indian culture as "squares" and "circles," the white men imposing unnatural straight lines and right angles on the roundness of nature. Now he points out that, despite the solid lines and diamond (square), baseball also embraces the roundness that the Indians identify with life: "Think of the circles instead of the lines—the ball, the circumference of the bat, the outfield running to the circle of the horizon, the batter running around the bases. Baseball is as close to the circle of perfection as white men are allowed to approach" (177-78).

The cornerstone of Drifting Away's religion is something found prominently with Black Elk, namely a "power vision"—a personal prophecy from the grandfathers, the revelation of a game not yet invented. The vision was given to him as a fifteen-year-old, as he was raised to the sky by hawks, raptured like J. D. Salinger in *Shoeless Joe*. While the boy did not yet understand the significance of the vision for his life, he did comprehend the sacred nature of the game: "'But the land above the river, above the holy tree, was staked out with sacred markings, and men were stationed about like ants….' 'It *is* a very holy business,' I said to the grandfathers. 'But there are white men doing the ceremony. Will they learn our ways? Have we become one people with them?'" (180).

In its synthesis of circles and squares, baseball might be capable of making whites and Indians one people, but it does not come about in Big Inning. Rather, what unites them is their obsessive nature: it leads to the apocalypse, and it is that which "the powers that be" wish to eradicate in the flood. Drifting Away, as the author's mouthpiece, explains the disaster in his answer to Gideon's question: "'Then what causes all this?' I wave a mud-encrusted hand to show I mean the flood and the endless game. 'Pride,' says Drifting Away. 'What else?' 'Is it so bad not to be moved? To stand by what you believe, no matter what? To have an obsession?' 'It is when obsession overrides love, takes precedence over brotherhood'" (270).

Brotherhood is evident on a small scale when Drifting Away rescues Gideon and when Gideon returns the favor. The Indian is about to pinch-hit on behalf of the Confederacy, and if he wins the game he regains his wife while Gideon loses Sarah. A struggle ensues as Drifting Away approaches the plate, but instead of clubbing the downed Indian and keeping Sarah, Gideon defers to his respected rival. "His quest has been so much longer than mine; he has suffered so much more.... I had my chance to end his quest, and by doing so to fulfill mine. But I couldn't do it" (286). Given another chance by Gideon, Drifting Away, once again "larger than life" (284) as he wields his unique bat—a root from the holy tree—hits a mighty home run that gives the underdog Confederacy, the "Indians," the victory. Perhaps as a tribute to his faithfulness and steadfastness, some power from beyond space-time intercedes to make his hit a game-winner. "The ball soars as if it has a life of its own, as if it has grown feathers, and like a white dove it flies toward infinity" (286).

The baseball as dove links the Indian religion and Drifting Away's power vision with a prominent biblical image. As symbol for the Holy Spirit, the dove fulfills ironically what Elder Womple had proclaimed earlier: "The very air is charged with the Spirit" (204). It also recalls the suggestion that Drifting Away is something of a messiah, a savior who restores loved ones to life, for the dove lighting on Christ in the River Jordan was a sign of his divine sonship and of God's pleasure (cf. Luke

3:22). Finally, as in Genesis, the dove signals the end of the flood and the restoration of the earth.[8]

The Holy Tree

Before that can come about, there is the final judgment of Big Inning and its obsessions. The town and several poor souls have been washed away, with the last things to go being Elder Womple, the Twelve-Hour Church, and the holy tree beside the river. The tree has proven to be the central image in the novel, and further analysis of it reveals many more facets of Kinsella's apocalyptic vision.

Like the city of Jerusalem, which is both a physical and spiritual focal point—and source of conflict—for three world religions, the holy tree embodies the passions and obsessions of the Indian and Christian sects in Big Inning, and, to a lesser degree, of the baseball religionists as well. They are all as firmly "rooted" in their convictions as is the tree by the river. Thus, the development of the apocalypse is reflected in the fate of the tree and its related images.

Gideon describes in detail the unique, impressive tree:

> It is a banyan-like tree, perhaps just a hearty weeping willow, but with a trunk that must be fifteen feet in diameter. I don't know enough mathematics to calculate the circumference. It is perhaps thirty feet tall, shaped like an umbrella with many long limbs lifted skyward, but

---

[8] A baseball is also pictured as a dove in *The Natural*, a novel that shares other imagery with *The IBC*. "He saw the ball spin off Roy's fingertips and it reminded him of a white pigeon he had kept as a boy, that he would send into flight by flipping it into the air. The ball flew at him and he was conscious of its bird-form and white flapping wings, until it suddenly disappeared from view" (28). The same image is employed in *Spitballs and Holy Water*.

heavy limbs, themselves as thick as ordinary tree trunks. And from each limb, at about five-foot-intervals, a new trunk grows straight down until it reaches the earth, where it takes root. The tree has expanded until it is a small forest itself, a labyrinth. (220)

This tree becomes a metaphor for Kinsella's view of world religions. There is one enormous trunk—equivalent to "the powers that be"—from which all others ultimately spring. The major religions, believing that they stand independently, are the limbs "as thick as ordinary tree trunks." However, they soon generate offshoots—sects—which themselves assume the form of an autonomous, self-sustaining tree (i.e., religion). They do not grow out, as a branch of the parent limb, but down, where they take root on their own and refuse to be moved. The expansion of religion through the proliferation of these stubborn sects has created the "labyrinth" of dogma and obsession, which Kinsella sees as the bane of human existence.

The Indians first called the tree "holy," but unlike other holy trees, it was not cut down, burned, and recycled after worship. Instead, it was deemed "too holy to cut…. It must be worshiped where it stands. Here we shall live, put down roots like this tree" (219). (These words echo the pronouncements both of Elder Womple, "We'll build our church on this spot" [190], and of Black Elk's vision of the leafy cottonwood as a symbol of life and prosperity: "Here we shall raise our children and be as little chickens under the mother sheo's wing" [34].) Because Drifting Away accepted his elder's designation of the tree as holy, he chose to build his tepee next to it and "would not be moved" (219). Then, in avenging the death of his wife, he massacred the whites under the sacred tree after ritualistically mixing his blood with its sap.

The church members do not call the tree "holy"—they refer to it as "the Indian tree" (134)—but they do incorporate it into their worship ritual, walking around it with white choir robes and candles. This activity reflects the words of their hymn: "Your blazing lamps raise bright and high / On every signal tree" (133). The hymn's other reference to the tree cites its location and its significance: "Like a tree / That's planted by the water / I shall not be moved" (134). Once again, there is a biblical passage, which is parodied in the depiction of Big Inning religion. The godly man is described in Psalm 1:3 as "a tree planted by the rivers of water, that bringeth forth his fruit in his season," but the tree at Big Inning produces only ungodly fruit.

Snaky Roots and Lightning Bolts

As the flood rises, the significance of the tree centers on the image of its roots. As a representation of intransigence, they continue to be assailed by the "malevolent" (284) waters, which aim to uproot religious obsession. The roots of the holy tree (and of others) are also equated with snakes or black eels, agents of destruction that churn violently in the flood.

When Bad News Galloway runs to his death as if possessed, "he throws himself into the water, which is full of tree roots thrashing like snakes in a moat." Discovered later downstream, Galloway's body has "a long, whiplike root coiled around its neck" (265). Likewise, when Gideon, determined to sacrifice himself for Drifting Away, is drawn to the holy tree, roots grasp at his legs, and one wraps itself around his back to cradle him in death. Then Drifting Away's rescue of Gideon thwarts the deadly attempts of the roots, which fight back: "As he swims through the eddying water, snakelike roots boil about us like eels, pulling us down with murderous intent. Drifting Away produces a knife and slashes us free, and we escape the free-flowing current. Is it my imagination, or are the detached roots writhing in pain, bleeding dark fluid into the river?" (269).[9]

The idea of roots as apocalyptic agents of the powers that be is reinforced by their connection to lightning.[10] Earlier, of course, lightning was the divine agent that had transmitted the history of the IBC to Matthew Clarke. It did so under another tree with displayed human qualities, one that screamed as lightning ripped off a limb and stunned Matthew. A similar response is elicited from nature when lightning appears on the twenty-first day of the game: "the cry of earth or tree, animal-like shrieks, death cries like rusty nails being pulled from a plank" (234).

Important, too, is the description of the lightning as "snake tongues shooting out of the cold, white sky" (234). The crowd of Twelve-Hour Church members, praying in tongues with hands raised above their heads in praise, proclaims, "Lightning is God's instrument!" (235). Here, as in the final stages of the flood, Kinsella is linking several motifs of divine intervention, such that something like the following equation takes shape: Roots = Snakes = Snake Tongues/Prayer Tongues = Lightning = God's Instrument, that is, both the roots and the lightning are God's instruments, or at least instruments of the apocalyptic powers that be.

However, instead of "fighting sin and Satan" (236), as the churchgoers' hymn would have it, the lightning attacks first the sacred tree, then Bob

---

[9] The almost human attributes of the tree, which bleeds and feels pain, were also seen earlier. As Drifting Away prepared himself to massacre the settlers, he cut the tree and himself to mix the sap with his blood. The drops of sap "appeared like tears in the wound" (191).

[10] Lightning is another important image also found in *The Natural*. For example, Roy Hobbs's magical bat was made from a "tree near the river where I lived [which] was split by lightning" (69). Of course, Drifting Away's bat is also from a "tree near the river," the holy tree. Root and snake imagery is also prominent in *The Seventh Babe*, and a powerful root doctor appears in *Things Invisible to See*. In *Havana Heat*, lightning shooting through the magic palm grove invests Dummy Taylor's reverie with a cultic power.

Grady, the Confederacy right fielder, who is borne aloft in the ascension or rapture parody mentioned above. The tree resists the lightning with as much determination as it does the floodwaters, and the battle that ensues amounts to a war between rival gods: "The tree shrieks again, repelling the lightning, the force of it, the essence of it, gathering like a molten metal sun in the upper branches. Then, like Zeus pitching lightning bolts, the tree draws itself back like a giant catapult and fires the coiled lightning back at the sky" (236).

The lightning adds to the apocalyptic imagery of the flood with a specific attack on the tree as the symbol of human obsession and intolerance. When the tree responds, it is as if the religions that exert their force over man are refusing to relinquish their power and have even added a fourth member, namely Zeus, the greatest of the ancient Greek gods. The resistance, however, is doomed to fail, as the lightning, the flood, and the snake-like roots in the floodwaters consummate the destruction. When finally the town, the church, and the holy tree are uprooted and washed away, only the bleachers and backstop at the ball field remain. Like the remnant on the ark, baseball is to be spared, to live on in future generations.

Drifting Away and Gideon are also spared, of course. The sacrifice by both men is the source of hope that outlasts the destruction of Big Inning. By leading the Confederacy to its victory, Drifting Away prevailed in the struggle with the grandfathers and thus fulfilled the conditions of their agreement. The end of the novel shows us that he has been reunited with his beloved wife, with whom he shares a life of relatively contented retirement on a reservation near Big Inning, now renamed Onamata.

Gideon's quest has been suspended by the deaths of Sarah and Sunny, but he appears to have learned a lesson about patience and obsession. Like Faust, he is finally contented with the pleasures of this world, specifically the love and joy of his neighbor, the feeble-minded Missy Baron, to whom he wishes to be a friend and guardian until her death. Yet there is hope that, after she is gone, he will be able to reclaim his great love, Sarah. The blending of his shadow with the headdress and profile of Drifting Away on the novel's last page indicates their oneness, their brotherhood, and his ability to defeat time after all—not with pride and obsession, but with love.

Appendix to Chapter 7
Three Religions in Conflict in The Iowa Baseball Confederacy

	Judeo-Christian	Small-Town American	American Indian
God	Jehovah	Baseball; Knowledge of the IBC	Grandfathers
Institution	Twelve-Hour Church of Time Immemorial	The Game— Inspired by God, arranged by the grandfathers	Being a worthy warrior
Scripture, Revelation	*The Holy Bible*	*A Short History of the IBC*	Power vision and promise from grandfathers
How Revealed	mountain top encounters, divine inspiration	Bolt of lightning	Encounter with grandfathers in the sky
Prophet(s)	Moses, Gideon, et al; Elder Womple	Abner Doubleday; Matthew and Gideon Clarke	Drifting Away
Sacred Ground	Church	Ball field	Iowa countryside
Holy Symbol(s)	Tree	Bat, ball grandstand	Tree
Shape of World	Squares, straight lines; resistance to nature	Harmony of squares and circles; straight and curved lines on the ball field	Circles, curved lines, harmony with nature
Paradise	Iowa, Heaven	Making the big leagues; loving Sarah	Nature; life with Onamata
Obsession	Life 12 hours off rest of world; keeping land; "We shall not be moved"	Learning the story of the IBC; winning the game; keeping Sarah; catching Sunny	Keeping land; reunion with deceased wife

Inning 8:

The Brothers K: An American Family Saga

Telling a Story

David James Duncan's *The Brothers K* is by far the longest novel in our study, a literary tour de force that is difficult to grasp but most rewarding when one does so. My engineer friends poke fun at themselves for always wanting to take things apart to figure out how they work…or why they don't. I reply that I feel like one of them when encountering certain novels—I'm fascinated and want to understand what makes them tick. Taking things apart, starting with the details of their construction, helps me, a "literary engineer" as it were, to understand and appreciate them more. As with *Things Invisible to See* and *Havana Heat*, I have done that with *The Brothers K*, whose structure, writes one reviewer, "appears rather ramshackle" (*Publishers Weekly*). It isn't, actually, and I hope that outlining the basics of

the novel will make it more accessible to other readers who might otherwise shy away from such a hefty tome.

Of course, it is not merely the length of *The Brothers K* that makes it such a challenge and delight, but also its rich mixture of characters and themes. Discussion of the book typically highlights three of them—baseball (which unifies the Chance family, protagonists of the novel), religion (specifically Seventh Day Adventism, the author's childhood faith, which divides them), and the Vietnam War—and all are essential. Yet Duncan is not writing "about" a particular theme as much as he is trying to tell a story, infused with slices of life and glimpses of the human condition. The author doesn't deny the numerous autobiographical details in his work (closeness to nature, an athlete father, a family divided over religion), but, like W. P. Kinsella, he rejects attempts to create "autobiographical links" back to the author. Such efforts, he maintains, tend to corrupt the reader's imagination and lessen the aesthetic pleasure of the reading experience. Instead, Duncan casts light through the prism of his own experience to "tell a story that *feels* true" (Lamberton 32). For instance, he initially intended to set his story among Baptists but realized that he lacked the firsthand experience to be credible. He reverted to the Adventists not to document his own family's story,[1] but to create something that "feels true."

Along with *Things Invisible to See*, *The Brothers K* may contain the least game action of any book in our study, but baseball, like religion, is so woven into the fabric of the novel that it is a natural for a book on "the great god Baseball." We have discussed how unfair and shortsighted it is of many crit-

---

[1] Duncan reports that his mother believed that all books amount to autobiography, and she felt that he had distorted the family's history. Only when a staunch Adventist friend assured her that Duncan had written an excellent novel, not a malicious exposé of her family, did the mother consent to finish it (Lamberton 33).

ics to dismiss good literature as simply "a baseball book," and perhaps nowhere is this truer than with Duncan's novel, an elaborate weave that does not reveal its essence at first glance. When we understand the basics of the novel's structure, it is easier to step back and view the big picture created by Duncan. What we see is neither autobiography, nor baseball book, nor religious treatise, nor war story. Instead, the colorful narrative threads yield a twentieth-century tapestry: an elaborate depiction of life in a large family and the constant tension between the centripetal and centrifugal forces of togetherness and separation. Much like *The Brothers Karamazov*, the nineteenth-century Russian classic echoed in Duncan's title, *The Brothers K* is ultimately a family saga, "the story of an eight-way tangle of human beings, only one-eighth of which was a pro ballplayer" (274).

Here are the eight members of the Chance family:

(1) Papa Hugh is a frustrated ballplayer whose pitching career was halted when an industrial accident crushed his thumb. Trying to throw again, he nails a mattress to the garage wall beyond a specially constructed pitching shed and begins obsessively to thump ball after ball against the padding. After a big toe is surgically transplanted to his hand, his pitching improves, which leads to a highly improbable comeback as a legendary minor-league pitcher and coach, even "a cup of coffee" in the big leagues. A longtime smoker, he dies early of lung cancer.

(2) Mama Laura became a devout Adventist when the church met urgent childhood needs that are only partly revealed to her family and the reader. Not until the end of the novel do we learn the terrible secret she is hiding. Her greatest wish is that her husband and children be firm in the

faith, but increasingly she alienates them with her fanaticism and violent outbursts.

(3) Everett, the eldest Chance child, is the most rebellious. He rejects and mocks the family's faith, engages in radical politics at college, and flees to Canada as a draft dodger during the Vietnam War. His revealing reflections on life are inserted as narrative interludes in the novel.

(4) Peter, the second child, is attracted by eastern culture and religion. He travels to Harvard for college and to India to become a Buddhist monk.

(5) Irwin makes a significant contribution to the narrative with his high school essay, "History of My Dad From His Birth Up To Kincaid's," reproduced in eight installments in books 1 and 2. The most devout of the children, Irwin wishes to register as a conscientious objector during the war, but the local congregation betrays him and he is drafted.[2] Because he attacks a superior officer in Vietnam, Irwin is diagnosed as "psychotic and violent" (458) and subjected to electroshock therapy. A determined group of Adventists and family members rescues him from the military-run mental institution in southern California and brings him home for a long but ultimately successful recovery.

(6) Kincaid (Kade), the youngest son, is the primary narrator of *The Brothers K*. He supplements his own account of the family with letters, jour-

---

[2] During the Civil War, noncombatancy was a requirement for membership and remained the official position of the church into the 1960s. "The Viet Nam War, however, provoked many Adventist young people to question the church's noncombatant position and, after considerable controversy, the General Conference's Autumn Council voted in 1969 to support those Adventists who sought to gain recognition as conscientious objectors" (Land "Noncombatancy"). Consequently, it was logical to expect that Irwin would have the full support of the church in his application for C. O. status.

nals, and reports from other observers, which simultaneously verify his account and give it variety.

(7 & 8) Bet and Freddy, twin sisters, are the youngest of the Chance children. Their role in the novel is much smaller than their brothers' role, though Bet does contribute a letter and a school report to the narrative.

Outer Structure: The Narrative Elements of The Brothers K

The Chances' story comprises 645 pages consisting of 6 books and 28 chapters, which are divided into mostly titled, mostly unnumbered segments, often bearing dates that range from 1956 to 1980. (One undated section includes a reference to the year 1985, the latest date in the book.) Many chapters are preceded by pithy epigraphs, including some from *The Brothers Karamazov*.

Brother Kade begins and ends his narration in the present tense. This suggests that the early text, though not labeled as such, may have been a youngster's journal or diary, with its repeated use of "now" and its naïve recounting of family banter. Kade refers to himself as "I," but it is not until page 16, when the father addresses him by name, that we know who "I" is. Book 1 continues in the present tense until it ends on page 100.

Book 2 immediately switches to a past tense narration, which is maintained through book 6, where Kade reveals that he has brought the reader up "to this day" (640). The last few pages of the novel are clearly an update, blending past and present tense, to conclude a family history that the narrator has pieced together in adulthood.[3] The book's last chapter is only a page long and written entirely in the present tense. It reprises the novel's

---

[3] Cf. Jackie Kapp's recollections of his coming of age with Christy Mathewson and the Giants in *The Celebrant*.

first page with almost the same wording, a loving father-son moment, but one generation later.

Kincaid's narration both moves the plot along, from one family member and episode to another, and provides continuity in the novel. One device he frequently uses is the summary of recent events, which helps the reader keep abreast of the increasingly divergent paths of the eight family members. There are about a half dozen of these summaries of varied length. Here is one example of the shortest: "While I became a pre-Feminist, Everett a pre-Hippie, Peter a pre-Bhikku, Bet and Freddy Famous Scientists, Grandawma a surprisingly fond memory and Papa one hell of a skilled backyard-mattress basher, Mama had also undergone a major change: she'd become a fanatic" (226). A longer summary section is found on pages 276-99, in which each Roman-numbered section updates one family member. There is another 4-line summary on page 369, one of 12 lines on page 382, and the final recap, character by character, on pages 641-43. As Kade chronicles the family's bonding, dissolution, and rebuilding over three decades, he reweaves the many unruly strands of the family history, pulling things together for himself and his family, and using these recaps to tie the novel together for the reader.

Interspersed in Kincaid's ongoing narration are the other narrative elements mentioned above: personal correspondence (about two dozen letters, postcards, and telegrams), children's school projects (by Irwin and Bet), a newspaper column (about Papa Chance's last game), entries from Everett's journal written while he was on the lam, and a medical transcript (of Irwin's condition). One chapter summarizes Kincaid's conversations with four veterans familiar with Irwin's trauma in Vietnam. Three times the extra-narrator accounts are labeled "Attic Documents," and one assumes that other materials are correspondence that never made it to the attic. Four undated passages by brother Everett (presumably written as Kincaid was organizing his retrospective) are positioned like interludes between books or chapters. Whether set off as separate sections or embedded in the text, these varied materials give the narrative the candor and poignancy one would expect from the naïve and often anguished children and young adults who wrote them.

Inner Workings: Tensions and Turning Points

An inner network of tensions and turning points in the "eight-way tangle" fleshes out the narrative structure of *The Brothers K*. There are too many to discuss in detail within the scope of this study, so I will select a few that, I trust, will help the reader track the development of the Chance family epic.

Imagine the Chances as a cluster of stars or planets, each one with gravitational forces connecting it to the others. One simple model of the family dynamics would be that of a solar system, with Papa Hugh as sun surrounded by Mama Laura and the children; seven lines of gravitational force connect him to the family. Papa is the basic reference point, the provider, and he's the focal point of Kincaid's early narrative and Irwin's long school essay. Dinnertime is oriented around his return home, and though he no longer likes to discuss it, everyone shares Papa's disappointment that he must earn his living in a hard, mindless mill instead of on a ball field. Interest in baseball, especially among the sons, connects everyone to Papa. Baseball's constant presence in conversation and on television is part of the air they breathe.

As the novel unfolds, a more accurate model would put father and mother at opposite poles of an axis. The parents, bound to each other in uneasy equilibrium, are surrounded by and connected separately to the six children,[4] the father via baseball, the mother via her religion; this yields thirteen lines of force, plus those between the children themselves, with "an astounding potential for complication" (151). Despite the parents' tensions, baseball and religion themselves are not seen as antagonistic in the novel. In fact, Papa Chance, with a Kinsella-like whimsy, comments that they have much in common. "Baseball and churches have got the same boredom factor, the same hypocrisy, the same Pie in a Big League Sky, the same bone-hard benches, the same loudmouthed yo-yos mixed in among the decent fans in the pews, the same power-loving preacher/managers delivering the same damned 'Do what I say or you're doomed' sermons. Hell, they've even got the same stinking organ music" (180).

The connections between parents and children are weakened as the children give up baseball and rebel against or drift away from the church. Those between the children, especially the sons, become problematic. Concern for each other is strong, but their differences increase as they grow older and seek their own identities. Taken together, these connections—or threads, if one will—illustrate why Kade calls the household an eight-way *tangle*. Family relationships are further complicated as the Chances encounter the social challenges of their era: drugs, extra-marital sex, radical politics, and war.

What gives the novel its great impact, its basic dynamic, is not just the *complexity* of these connections, but the crackling *tension* that courses through them—analogous to that between magnetic poles—which alternately attracts and repels, bonds and fractures. Such tension simmers

---

[4] Perhaps the standard physics illustration of iron shavings curved around the ends of a magnet is useful.

throughout the novel and is brought to a head in several episodes that we can designate as fateful turning points in the plot.

A. Father-Son Passions

One turning point is at the end of book 1, when Kade, hurt that his father isn't listening to him, speaks sharply and disrespectfully, provoking a hard punch to the face that Hugh Chance immediately and desperately regrets. What follows is one of the more moving father-son scenes in all of baseball literature. "Kade, I'm *sorry*! But what *is* it with you? What do you *expect* from me?" (99). Through his blood and sobs, the son cites the example of Vera, a young, harelipped girl at church who, despite her profound speech impediment, fearlessly offers fervent, if barely intelligible prayers. "I *know* you hate the mill," gasps Kade. "I *know* you love baseball, and aren't doing what you want. But at least Vera *fights*.... All I want is for *you* to fight, Papa. To fight to stay alive inside! No matter *what*" (99). Moved by his son's love and wisdom, Papa Chance accepts the challenge to live again.[5] The very next day, he shreds his cigarettes, dons sweat clothes, and begins to work himself back into shape. One week later, like Ray Kinsella in *Shoeless Joe*, he "insanely" begins to create part of a ballpark on his property, building the pitching shed, then a pitcher's mound, while Kade makes a batter's box. Initially, Papa won't admit to a Kinsella-like dream of a "fairytale comeback.... All I'm ever gonna do out here is toss the pitcher's equivalent of harelip prayers.... Call it my hobby, or some weird kind of worship maybe" (113). But Kade dreams. He raptly follows his father's earnest but

---

[5] I find this particularly moving, for it reminds me of a beloved uncle who, though tethered to an oxygen tank, continues to build additions to his home that he may never use and tries to patent an invention he may never see produced. People shake their heads at his eccentricities, but I see in my uncle a desire to *fight* and to *live*.

often helpless efforts, drawing ever closer to him: "The more he missed the mattress, the louder he blasted the bare wall, the fiercer and deeper my love for him grew" (118).

B. The End of Childhood

Hugh Chance's rebirth is compelling to follow, as Kade does from a hiding spot in the hedge and we do through him. The father's efforts, we realize, represent a "two-sided struggle to reconcile who he had been (the finest athlete a lot of people had ever seen) with who he had become (a millworking, shedball-playing father of six)" (156). However, reconciliation comes at a cost to the family, for Papa abandons the dinner hour and his standard, mumbled table grace to return to the pitching shed. The Chance children attempt to fill the void by alternately offering a mealtime prayer, but disaster comes when Everett provocatively and repeatedly prays, "Dear God, if there is One…if You exist" (168), and the like, provoking his mother to lash out physically, first against Everett, then against would-be peacemakers Irwin and Peter. Kade labels this horrendous scene "Psalm Wars" and interprets Mama's convulsive gasps as "the death rattle of my brothers' and my childhood" (170).

C. A Fork in the Trail

Later that year, Kincaid notes a parting of the ways among the brothers. Everett—"an ersatz bohemian skuzzball"—and Peter—"Camas, Washington's first self-made Buddhist monk" (206)—divide their shared bedroom into antagonistic camps. "Far more troubling than this visual tension," writes Kade, "was the unseen tension between the inhabitants" (206). The eldest Chance brothers had come to "a fork in the trail," a key image in this coming-of-age novel, leaving the youngest son standing "back at the fork, watching them veer farther and farther apart, and grieving for us all" (207).

D. Irwin's Predicament

Even as Papa Chance's pro baseball comeback is flourishing, Kincaid's next older brother, Irwin, the last he would expect to shake up the family, throws everyone a curve. In a dizzying few pages of book 4, chapter 3, he announces that (1) he wants to get married; (2) it must be tomorrow; (3) he and abused seventeen-year-old Linda are expecting a baby; (4) he has been drafted into the Army. As Irwin elaborates, the family further learns that he is destined for Vietnam, that their church sabotaged his application for Conscientious Objector status, and that the family must care for Linda and the baby while he is gone. These revelations, complicated by "Psalm Wars, Part Two," another slugfest with Everett, put the family into "some kind of dream-zone" (361) from which they spend the rest of the novel escaping. While they have many serious issues to work through, they begin to do it together, overcoming the centrifugal forces that spin them apart, and restoring, re-creating, their family.

About That Catchy Title

So, what about the clever title, *The Brothers K*? It has two meanings: the obvious reference to Fyodor Dostoevsky's masterpiece; and baseball scoring shorthand for "strikeout," which is "K." The literary allusion reveals many instructive parallels between Duncan's long novel and Dostoevsky's.[6] First,

---

[6] Duncan states that he learned how to write by "reading great, difficult books" and by imitating nineteenth-century writers such as Charles Dickens and Mark Twain (Lamberton 34). While he doesn't specifically name Dostoevsky as a mentor, his affinity to the Russian is apparent.

there is the narrative structure. *The Brothers Karamazov* consists of parts, books, and chapters, while *The Brothers K* is made up of books, chapters, and what I call interludes. Both novels are directed by a central narrator—anonymous and outside the plot in Dostoevsky, brother Kincaid in Duncan—but have other voices as well. Dostoevsky criticism typically calls this form "polyphonic," a term that is also appropriate for Duncan. Both writers prominently insert the narratives of other commentators, such as Ivan Karamazov's famous "Legend of the Grand Inquisitor" and Aloysha's "Life of Zosima," and the writings of Irwin and Everett Chance noted above.

Each novel features four rather different brothers whose primary reference point, for good or ill, is their father. Of *Karamazov*, Margot K. Frank writes that the author "has the major characters respond in different ways to their situation, developing each in terms of a specific psychological or metaphysical problem" (515), and the same holds true for *The Brothers K*. There is no one-to-one correspondence between the two sets of brothers, and they are from two different worlds, but they are comparably involved in grappling with the issues of life and society: "Like Dostoevsky's Karamazovs, the Chances speculate on the nature of God, delve into the nuances of what constitutes moral behavior, experience evil, suffer from criminal acts, and, finally, determine that God is love and love redeems" (Michaud 172).

No mother is present in *Karamazov*; the father's long shadow falls over the entire plot, creating sparks—war, really—in the sons' relationship to him and to each other. In Duncan's novel by contrast, the brothers' relationship to their father is generally positive, and there *is* a mother present. The sparks in this family—which also develop into wars, called "Psalm Wars"—arise from a religious zeal that pits her first against her husband, then against her sons. In both books, the brothers differentiate themselves in their family roles and in their observations on and participation in the social maelstrom that swirls around them. The debates that take place face to face among the Karamazovs are shifted to another plane among the Chances, as narrator Kade creates his debates through the collected memoirs. Finally, in both books the father's passing removes major conflict from the family and permits the rebirth.

Both Dostoevsky and Duncan have their roots in a strict religious upbringing, the former in Russian Orthodoxy, the latter in Seventh Day Adventism, and both have a strong religious component to their plot. Each takes as a motto a biblical passage that could relate to both novels. *Karamazov*'s epigraph is John 12:24, "I tell you the truth, unless a kernel of wheat falls to the ground and dies, it remains only a single seed. But if it dies, it produces many seeds." That verse could reflect the novel's cyclical narrative structure, as one critic has asserted,[7] or it could suggest the healing and regeneration in Fyodor's seed after he and his murderer, Smerdyakov, have died. The theme of resurrection is also prominent in *The Brothers K*, initially when Papa Chance's career dies and is reborn with the toe transplant, and later when the fractured family regroups after his death.

The key Bible verse of *The Brothers K* is Matthew 10:36, "a man's enemies will be the members of his own household." Here, Jesus is predicting how people will be at odds over his claims to lordship, with some accepting and others rejecting them, and this holds true in the context of the fragmenting Chance family. There, however, it is less the person of Christ that is at issue than the dogmas of Adventism and the quirks of the local congregation and its leader, Elder Babcock. The "man" of verse 36 is Hugh

---

[7] Robin Feuer Miller, quoted in Knapp 139.

Chance, whose enemy is primarily his wife, Laura. But "man" can also be read as "person," and Laura is on a war footing with not only her husband but her sons as well, above all Everett. The family is also split in their attitudes toward the Vietnam War, and to a certain extent they are a microcosm of the extended family of American society, which fractured over the war. Just as clearly, the verse from Matthew applies to Dostoevsky as it portrays the parricidal sentiments of the Karamazov brothers.

A central reference point for both family sagas is, perhaps surprisingly, given the family tensions they depict, a happy childhood. In his "Speech at the Stone," reflecting on the death of a youngster, Dostoevsky's Alyosha maintains:

> You must know that there is nothing higher and stronger and more wholesome and good for life in the future than some good memory, especially a memory of childhood, of home. People talk to you a great deal about your education, but some good, sacred memory, preserved from childhood, is perhaps the best education. If a man carries many such memories with him into life, he is safe to the end of his days, and if one has only one good memory left in one's heart, even that may sometime be the means of saving us (820).

Kincaid Chance, in an early part of his memoir, is not nearly so sophisticated: "When you get right down to it, it's a great family I got. But then it's easy to love everybody the same amount when they're your family" (39). The reader senses that this kinship, anchored in love, was present not only in Kade's childhood but also in his middle age. It undergirds his effort to reconstruct the family history and reflects the contentment that marks the reconciled family.

The other aspect of Duncan's catchy title is the baseball scoring symbol for strikeout, "K," which is exposited in a brief but highly charged segment that in effect functions as an epigraph to book 5, "The Brothers K." The text, titled "A Definition" and written as a dictionary entry, is the last of Everett Chance's four interludes, and the most telling. We will examine it in detail below, after first summarizing the previous three interludes.

These writings constitute Everett's retrospective on three decades in which the Chance family saga unfolds. They contribute significant insights into that turbulent era, but increasingly they constitute Everett's coming to terms with himself. The four interludes begin with "Roger Maris, Radical of the Sixties," inserted as a prelude to chapter 1 of book 4. Everett's (Duncan's) unusual interpretation of the Yankee star who broke Babe Ruth's home run record in 1961 is that Maris gave up all-around baseball excellence for the narrow, intensely focused purpose of hitting home runs. This focus Everett calls a "technical obsession" (273), comparable to what characterizes highly successful people like Charles Darwin or Robert Oppenheimer. "Obsession works" (272), he writes, but, as in several other baseball novels, it brings with it "an overpowering, malignant magic" (274). This magic, though it created for Maris extraordinary success, cost him his humanity and brought "confusion and regret" (274). Obsession is also a trait of the Chances, witness Everett's own addictions as a high-profile campus radical, Papa Hugh's feverish baseball comeback, and Mama Laura's religious fanaticism.

The second interlude, called "Renunciation," is found between chapters 1 and 2 of book 4. It takes issue with brother Peter's renunciation of his family, religion, and culture in favor of Buddhism and Eastern thought, for he believes Peter gave up nothing with which he was comfortable. Instead, Everett attributes Peter's renunciation to an effort "to outsmart his pain" (303) and "question[s] his calculations: to slough off half a self in hopes of finding a whole one is not my idea of good math" (304). The painful search for the self is a prominent one with most of the characters in *The Brothers K*, and it emerges below as a key to Everett's conclusions.

The third interlude, set between chapters 2 and 3 of book 4, is called "Three Kinds of Farce" ("The Genre," i.e., the dramatic form derived from Aristophanes, "Megafarce," and "Microfarce"). Everett labels as "Megafarce" the post-World War II activities of the US government and military in the Cold War, and as "international Megafarce" the Vietnam War. In explaining the effect of these forces on the American people and how they moved him to radicalism, Everett also touches on the essence of the novel, namely the struggles of a family and the growing pains of its members: "Strong families like mine kept fighting for a family identity, and strong characters like my brothers and sisters still struggled to come of age in nonfarcical ways. But our lives were being violated, trivialized, and in tens of thousands of cases terminated by the trite machinations of these sickeningly powerful men" (352).

In trying to combat the Megafarce of the sixties and seventies, Everett became, he confesses, a "Microfarce," obsessed with fame and sex. Idolized for his speaking skills, dubbed by fellow radicals the "Hippie Churchill," he became a caricature of a great orator, unable to stop performing and relate honestly to people. As with Darwin, Oppenheimer, and Maris, obsession robbed him of his humanity and "sent him fleeing in panic" (354) when he looked at himself and saw an "aching, self-doubting, harrowingly unfunny stranger" (354). Having rejected the script of the Megafarce, he created his own, the Microfarce, but the result was the same: he was trapped in a script, "prepackaged, programmed, pinned to a page. Only the unwritten can truly live a life," he asserts. "So who I was, what I was, had to be unwritten" (355).

This is an astounding admission for the most rebellious of the brothers Chance and sets up the final installment of Everett's interludes, the stunning dictionary definition that follows:

K (ka) *verb*, K'ed, K'ing. **1.** *baseball*: to strike out. **2.** to fail, to flunk, to f—-up, to fizzle, or **3.** to fall short, fall apart, fall flat, fall by the wayside, or on deaf ears, or hard times, or into disrepute or disrepair, or **4.** to come unglued, come to grief, come to blows, come to nothing, or **5.** go to the dogs, go through the roof, go home in a casket, go to hell in a hand basket, or **6.** to blow your cover, blow your chances, blow your cool, blow your stack, shoot your wad, bitch the deal, buy the farm, bite the dust, only **7.** to recollect an oddball notion you first heard as a crimeless and un-K'ed child but found so nonsensically paradoxical that you had to ignore it or defy it or betray it for decades before you could begin to believe that it might possibly be true, which is that **8.** to lose your money, your virginity, your teeth, health or hair, **9.** to lose your home, your innocence, your balance, your friends, **10.** to lose your happiness, your hopes, your leisure, your looks, and, yea, even your memories, your vision, your mind, your way,

11. in short (and as Jesus K. Rist once so uncompromisingly put it) to lose your very self,

12. for the sake of another, is

13. sweet irony, the only way you're ever going to save it (380).

This passage, arguably the meatiest of the book, resembles a poem in its ability to express so much in so few words. It is placed like an epigraph before the longest chapter, with about one third of the novel yet to come. Like many an epigraph, it hints at what is to come or sounds a tone to set the pitch, but it also functions much like one of Kincaid's summaries, written as it was at least five years after the end of the novel's recorded events. However, instead of summarizing actions character by character, it extrapolates (if obliquely) Everett's own experiences into the novel's commentary on life. Let us here consider in sequence the dictionary entry's thirteen "definitions" (is Everett superstitious?); they are a linguistic delight and a nugget of wisdom.

1. The baseball definition of K as a verb, to strike out. The subsequent variations are an alliterative compilation of synonyms for failure, negative situations that people in their folly create and suffer through. Everett does not write in the first person, but the negatives do fit the circumstances of his life. The definitions can apply to all people, yet it is fair to assume that Everett primarily implicates himself. Points 2-5 all conclude with "or," indicating equivalency with the following definition.

2-3. More alliteration. Five different verbs beginning with "f." Definition 3 gives eight uses of "fall."

4. Four negative verb constructions beginning with "come."

5. Four examples of ruin with the word "go."

6. Four constructions beginning with "blow," followed by "shoot your wad" and three more verbs beginning with "b." Significantly, the last word in this definition is "only," which breaks with the dictionary format and establishes the passage as something of a narrative as it connects to definition 7.

7. Reflects on one's unspoiled ("un-K'ed") youth, when life was anchored by a particular "oddball notion" against which one rebelled. Everett uses increasingly stronger verbs—"ignore," "defy," and "betray"—to

define the rebellion before conceding that the notion, which had seemed "nonsensically paradoxical…might possibly be true." The "notion" is perhaps that God, family, and country—the things Everett most rebelled against—are greater than the individual and greatly to be valued, but Everett defines it more sublimely, after linking definition 7 to 8 by the words "which is that," thus continuing the narrative.

8-10. Variations on the word "lose," seventeen in all.

11-13. All indented, setting them apart from the previous meanings of "K" to highlight Everett's biblical conclusion as he paraphrases well-known words of Jesus Christ. (In a residual bit of irreverence, as if not to appear totally to have "sold out," Everett spells the name Jesus K. Rist). Jesus' words are "Whoever finds his life will lose it, and whoever loses his life for my sake will find it" (Matt 10:39; also, with little variation in wording [e.g., "save," "love," or "keep" for "find" and "hate" for "lose"], Mark 8:35, Luke 9:24, and John 12:25). Everett's paraphrase takes only the second half of Jesus' lesson: where the biblical verb sequence is "find…lose…lose…find," Everett's is just "lose…find." He also modifies the wording from "for my [i. e., Jesus'] sake" to "for the sake of another," thus substituting the horizontal person-person relationship for the vertical person-God one. He does this by blending two verses, Matthew 10:39 et al., which we have been considering, and John 15:13, which reads "Greater love has no one than this, that he lay down his life for his friends."

Everett's biblical paraphrase, which amounts to the lesson that he has taken decades to learn, has two fascinating antecedents, the first being the Dostoevsky connection. Recall that *The Brothers Karamazov* bore the paradoxical epigraph of John 12:24, that one must die in order to live. The following verse, 25, is the one on which Everett seizes, the equally paradoxical assertion of John that one must lose oneself to find oneself.

The other antecedent of Everett's "K" definitions is, of course, his previous text, which the narrator, Kade, has inserted as interludes at three other places in the novel. As we saw, the third interlude concludes with the insight that led him to the biblical paraphrase: "Only the unwritten can truly live a life. So who I was, what I was, had to be unwritten" (355). It is this being "unwritten"—losing oneself, in effect—that culminates in the dictionary definitions of "K." There Everett gives seventeen instances of "losing" in life and ties them to the biblical injunction to lose oneself to find oneself. It concludes Everett's text and gives closure to his part of the family saga.

Written as it is at least five years after the rest of Kade's narrative (though placed much earlier in the novel), it also caps off the entire family's coming of age. Closure for the rest of the Chances is provided in several events consistent with the theme of death and rebirth in John 12:24-25. When Papa Chance faces death from cancer, his children draw together, see Irwin returned from a living death, and, in a stunning revelation only pages from the book's end, understand for the first time the source of their mother's travails: as a young child, she was sexually molested by her father. Repeatedly betrayed each time she tried to report the continuing abuse, Laura finally found sanctuary among the Adventists, who spirited the family to a safe location away from the father. When the old man died driving drunk, it confirmed Laura's belief in the power of prayer.

As Peter writes this news to Everett, he uses a term similar to Everett's "unwritten" self: "Our entire relationship with Mama is being unmade" (634). The new relationship of love and understanding brings Peter "the very mother I've always longed for," and "even her theology makes sense to me now" (635). "We'll be years sorting this out" (635), Peter adds, but the healing of a fractured family is well underway. Kincaid's final summary documents the post-1970s status of the family. It shows that, though the "seed" of John 12:24 has fallen into the ground and died, Laura and her family now rejoice in the "many seeds" of Chance grandchildren.

Inning 9:

Evolving Dreams and Spiritual Mysteries in *Havana Heat*

As with Darryl Brock's breakthrough novel, *If I Never Get Back*, *Havana Heat* does a masterful job of transporting the reader to an earlier era, two eras, in fact. The novel is anchored in the framework narrative of a 1958 awards ceremony, just months before the death of its protagonist, Luther "Dummy" Taylor, a deaf, former pitcher for John McGraw's New York Giants. The bulk of the novel, the interior story, consists of Taylor's recollections of fall 1911, when the pitcher regains his arm strength and tries to begin a major league comeback on the Giants' postseason trip to Cuba.

As with so many of the works discussed in this study, we find that *Havana Heat* is much more than "just" a baseball novel. The richness of this book lies in the many threads of Dummy Taylor's story that weave a bittersweet tapestry of life and draw us into the lives of people we grow to care

much about: Taylor and his wife, Della; selected teammates, including McGraw, Christy Mathewson, and Mike Donlin; and the deaf youngsters and adults in the US and Cuba who are inspired by Taylor's accomplishments. The novel's unexpected punch, however, derives from the exotic prophecies, healings, and rites of the native folk religion known as *santería*. The power of *santería*, in something of an uneasy triangle with Taylor's nominal Protestantism and the Roman Catholicism of the Cuban priest who seeks out the Giants' pitcher for a special mission, mysteriously helps Taylor resolve the tensions in his life and fulfill his deepest yearning.

Readers of novelists who went before will hear echoes of their work in Darryl Brock's superb prose, but the allusions are light, the "influence" muted. Most obviously, *Havana Heat* shares with *The Celebrant* an uncanny recreation of American life in the early twentieth century and the intimate portrait of the same team, the storied New York Giants. Like *The Year the Yankees Lost the Pennant*, *Shoeless Joe*, and *The Brothers K*, it portrays a man trying to balance his wife's concerns for security with his own baseball dream. And, as in these other novels, the dream evolves and is fulfilled in different and surprising ways. Like *The Seventh Babe* and *Spitballs and Holy Water*, *Havana Heat* confronts the ugly social issues of racism and segregation, and with *The Iowa Baseball Confederacy* and *The Seventh Babe* it uses snake, tongue, and lightning imagery to link baseball games with apocalyptic and voodoo religious practices.

For all these similarities to his predecessors, however, Brock has created a unique work in both form and content. For instance, I am not aware of another baseball author who presents such a convincing portrayal of deaf culture, a central component of the novel. Moreover, the background information on Cuban independence from Spain, its racial politics, and the emerging tensions with the United States adds yet another dimension to the baseball and family stories. In this chapter we will touch on these themes as they contribute to the main analysis, but will not trace them in depth. Instead, we will concentrate on the book's carefully developed narrative structure and attempt to demonstrate how it shapes the religious reverie that does much to resolve Dummy Taylor's conflicts and fulfill his dreams.

Splendid Symmetry: The Narrative Structure of *Havana Heat*

Because the narrative structure of *Havana Heat* is so vital to an understanding of Dummy Taylor's story and because we will be examining it in some detail, I have included an outline of the novel as a footnote below.[1] There the reader will see that the book, as mentioned above, consists of two balanced narratives that complement each other well: a framework story, printed in italics, *about* Dummy Taylor in 1958 at his alma mater, the Kansas School for the Deaf, and an interior story *by* Taylor, a fictional first-

---

[1] *Havana Heat* **Outline.** Italics are used below for the five segments of the framework story, where Brock's text is italicized. The frame relates Taylor's thoughts at a 1958 awards ceremony, four months before his death.

1-4	*Prologue, Olathe, Kansas, April 1958*
5-101	Part 1: THE SIGN
7-32	Chapter 1, Baldwin, Kansas. October 1911
33-50	Chapter 2
51-72	Chapter 3
73-74	*Chapter 4, Olathe, 1958*
75-101	Chapter 5
103-79	Part 2: THE MOTION
105-15	Chapter 6
116-30	Chapter 7
131-43	Chapter 8
144-55	Chapter 9
156-57	*Chapter 10, Olathe, 1958*
158-70	Chapter 11
171-79	Chapter 12
181-244	Part 3: THE TARGET
183-98	Chapter 13
199-209	Chapter 14
210-28	Chapter 15
229-30	*Chapter 16, Olathe, 1958*
231-44	Chapter 17
245-99	Part 4: THE DELIVERY
247-69	Chapter 18
270-83	Chapter 19
284-99	Chapter 20
301-304	*Epilogue, Olathe, 1958*

person account of his exploits in the year 1911. The italicized framework, beginning in the prologue, shows how certain items displayed at a ceremony to honor him—his spikes and glove, a carved wooden figure, a magazine article on Cuba, a signed program—trigger Taylor's imagination and stimulate his recollections of 1911. "The images came" (4).

The interior story, too, reveals how sensitive Taylor is to images; they cause him to reflect on his family and childhood in Kansas, his career in baseball, and his marriage to Della. For example, when a neighbor shows him a newspaper picture previewing the upcoming World Series between the New York Giants and Philadelphia Athletics, Taylor is stunned. "As I stared at the picture, time seemed to stop. Then it seemed to jump backward.... That photo hit me like a sock to the belly" (11); "the image of the players in those dark uniforms would not go away" (14). Later, he comes upon a scrapbook his wife had compiled during the glory days, and "I made the mistake of opening it. As if guided by fate, the pages spread to reveal the picture Monte had shown me that morning. Except that this one had been taken six years ago" (19). Taylor, we learn, had been an important part of the Giants' 1905 pennant winner, but was passed over in the World Series. His baseball dream was sabotaged by the snub and by the sore arm that relegated him to the minor leagues, but now the "images," guided by "fate" and the renewed strength of his arm, move him to contemplate a comeback.

The body of the novel has four titled "parts," comprised of twenty untitled chapters. Three of the chapters belong to the 1958 frame, and seventeen of them make up the 1911 interior. The four parts are all preceded by an epigraph and titled in large, uppercase type. In each instance, the epigraph suggests a key issue of the part, and each title has two meanings: an obvious baseball connotation and a hidden reference to the emerging story. Moreover, the first three parts each contain a chapter of framework that introduces another key image or focuses Taylor's memory on a landmark event in his life. There is thus a symmetry both to the four parts and to the five italicized segments (prologue, chapters 4, 10, and 16, and epilogue) to which they relate.

The interaction between the two narratives, while perhaps not evident at first, is integral to the novel's development. It is particularly the framework that moves the novel forward. It introduces visual stimuli, images that are then interpreted in the interior. The images prompt the protagonist to call up his memories, and they prepare the reader, if only subconsciously, for the story to follow. The framework also answers questions—from the vantage point of forty-seven years of hindsight—that are raised by the events of the longer 1911 memoir. The questions (listed below[2]), create an ongoing suspense in the lives of the characters and thus the reader.

---

[2] The issues that produce tension in the novel derive from the characters' aspirations and dreams that fall roughly into three categories. From this dialectic spring numerous questions that produce a heightened interest in and anticipation of the story of Luther "Dummy" Taylor.

(1) HIS DREAM: A BASEBALL COMEBACK. Is his baseball career finished, or will his rejuvenated arm permit him to return to the Major Leagues? Will he be granted a tryout? How will his former manager and teammates receive him? How will his arm hold up under the pressure of the Cuban series? Will he succeed in Havana, and if so, will that lead to a contract for the next season?

(2) HER DREAM: LAND AND MARRIAGE. Will the Taylors' marriage survive the differences between them? Will Dummy continue to be bothered by Della's aging and less attractive appearance? Will she be further alienated by the memory of his earlier affair and the fear that he may not return to her from the barnstorming trip to Cuba? How will they relate to each other after he comes back? Will they ever have children, and how will childlessness affect their relationship? Will she get the additional land she dreams of?

(3) NEW DREAMS: THE CUBAN ADVENTURE. Why is the Cuban priest trying to contact Taylor? What is Luis's problem, and will the Giants pitcher be willing and able to help? How will Luis acquit himself in the tryout in Matanzas? To what extent will Taylor recover from being clubbed by a bat, and what role does the folk religion called *santería* play in his healing? To what do the prophecies refer? What is Taylor's secret plan, and will Manager McGraw agree to it? How will the Cuban youngsters respond to the challenge of playing the Giants? Will Luis pitch well enough to win himself a contract? Will his outlaw grandfather appear at the game, as Luis hopes? If so, how will it affect his performance and his future? How much of Taylor's final, profound encounter with *santería* is real and how much imagined? How does the experience alter his dream and shape his future? What happens to Luis, his family, and the youngster's baseball career?

What follows is a section-by-section elaboration of the two intertwined narratives as touched on above and outlined in footnote 89. In highlighting the recurring features of the two narratives, replete with the double entendres of epigraphs and titles, it aims to illustrate the splendid symmetry that distinguishes the structure of *Havana Heat*.

Prologue, Olathe, Kansas, April 1958—The *prologue*, discussed above, is the beginning of the italicized framework story. It launches the memoirs that make up the body of the novel.

Part 1: THE SIGN—The *epigraph* is a poem by Walt Whitman rejecting the joys of nature for the lure of the city, and concluding "Give me such shows—give me the streets of Manhattan!" (5). This, it turns out, presages Dummy Taylor's desire to return to New York and the tension with his wife, Della, who much prefers the Kansas prairie.

The *title* of part 1 is "The Sign," an apparent reference to the beginning of each pitching sequence, when a pitcher takes a sign from the catcher. The deeper meaning of this title emerges as Taylor wrestles with the question of his immediate future: "I stood there staring at the page, overcome by the feeling that I should be…where? I didn't know. But not there. Not in a hole in the middle of the damned Kansas prairie" (20). The answer comes after his impromptu prayer for direction: "I wasn't much of a churchgoer, except when Ma or Della dragged me, but at that moment I felt so bad that I said a sort of prayer to the snow. I asked for a sign, some direction to follow, something to ease my discontent" (84).[3] The following day the "sign"

---

[3] This sequence hints at Ray Kinsella's quest in *Shoeless Joe*, who stares at the snow on his unused ball field, constructed at the behest of a voice, and wonders when something will show him that he was correct to obey. It also ties Taylor's desire for "something to ease my discontent" to the voice's subsequent command, "ease his pain," meaning that Kinsella should seek out recluse author J. D. Salinger.

arrived, a telegram from the Giants offering a chance, however slim, for a comeback.

Chapter 4, Olathe, 1958—The *framework insert* in part 1 introduces another image that jogs Taylor's memory: a yellowed ball from a 1904 game in Chicago. "It had been his best day in the bigs" (73), something any former professional would remember. However, the dirt ground into the ball suggests the tension with his wife, who longed to purchase more land, dirt: "That ball represented the whole difference between them: her wanting him at home, tied to their property; him aching to be off in distant cities, breezing a seamed sphere past opponents with cunning and power" (74).

Part 2: THE MOTION—The *epigraph* here consists of two quotes, one of which, by baseball pioneer Henry Chadwick, suggests that the American pastime will have a civilizing, almost evangelizing effect on less advanced Latin culture: "The time was, and not five years ago, when the American game was nowhere an attractive game beside the brutal bull fights, but the people are becoming civilized, and when they do, base ball will supplant the heathenish sport" (103). Chadwick's remarks point to cultural differences between the Americans and Cubans, some of which are accentuated, others resolved by baseball, such as in the 1911 series between the Giants and the Cuban teams.

The *title* of part 2, "The Motion," denotes the next phase of the pitching sequence, the hurler's windup after taking the sign, and one could say that Taylor is "moving" toward Cuba in response to the sign he received through the telegram. Its deeper meaning, however, is the sensuality of Cuban culture—its music, food and drink, ardent baseball fans, and native religions—as encountered by North Americans such as Taylor. The "rolling water" (105) over which the Giants journey to Havana by ship creates an immediate sense of motion, as do later bedroom scenes, but the most direct subtext is the description of the Giants' musical welcome at the dock: "Massed onlookers gyrated to the music with hip-thrusting motions that would've landed them in the calaboose back in Baldwin" (107).

Chapter 10, Olathe, 1958—The *framework insert* in part 2 is suggested by Taylor's old spiked shoes, purchased by Della as a special gift to help his nascent career. They call to mind another memorable day, the one of their first lovemaking, but also a rift in the marriage, their lack of children.

Part 3: THE TARGET—The *epigraph* is a brief poem by the Cuban freedom fighter and martyr, José Martí: "To find you, son, / I cross the seas. / The kindly waves / Take me to you" (181). These words point to the ultimate purpose of Taylor's sea voyage to Cuba and his refocused dream, not to make a major league comeback but to mentor Luis, the deaf pitching sensation, and "sire" many more sons in his coaching career.

The *title* of part 3 is "The Target," which on the surface refers to the catcher's glove, the focal point of a pitcher's motion toward the plate. Instead, the target could be young Luis, who is the as yet unknown target of Taylor's quest, or even Taylor himself, who is singled out by local religious figures to mentor Luis.

Chapter 16, Olathe, 1958—The brief *framework insert* in part 3 is triggered by a 1905 World Series program signed by the players and by the deaf fans who had followed Taylor. Their signatures call to mind two more milestones in the pitcher's life: first, the mutual inspiration that Taylor and his fans had been to each other, which gave him "the feeling that he was playing for more than himself" (229); second, "More than anything else after leaving the game, he had missed the endless pranks and plots and friendships—hell, even the quarrels—that went into the camaraderie of being part of a team" (230).

Part 4: THE DELIVERY—The final part's *epigraph* comes from an American cultural text written in 1911, the year of the interior story. Its comment that the "enumerators who took the census under our military occupation acknowledged the difficulty of distinguishing among a people whose prevailing physical characteristics are dark skin and black hair" (245) illustrates the racism that trumps the sensational pitching performance by Luis, Dummy Taylor's deaf Cuban protégé. Taylor and the Giants wish to sign the light-skinned Luis for the Major Leagues, but when the boy's black grandfather appears at the game, they realize that racial politics will make it impossible to do so.[4]

The *title* of part 4, "The Delivery," refers at one level to the end of the sequence, when the pitcher releases or "delivers" the ball. Its subtext is the fulfillment of Taylor's dream, the "delivery" of a son. When Taylor uses the word "son" in a general sense to encourage Luis during the game, the boy takes it more literally. "And suddenly I found myself wishing he was my son. I'd have given anything for a boy like him. Right then I felt as close to Luis Serros Avelar as if he were my flesh and blood" (272). He's not, of course, but Luis and hundreds more deaf boys do become like sons in the coaching career of Dummy Taylor.

Epilogue, Olathe, 1958—There is no italicized insert within part 4, but the *epilogue* returns us to the framework, ties off the loose threads of the two narratives, and completes the novel. We learn that Della got her land and Dummy his surrogate sons; that Taylor married twice more after Della's death, women "deaf like the others, childless like the others" (302); that the 1912 "Black Uprising" in Cuba, which sought equal rights for

---

[4] In fact, two light-skinned Cuban blacks, Armando Marsans and Rafael Almeida, were signed in 1911 by the Cincinnati Reds. According to Robert Peterson, this created "a minor furor in the National League" and raised "new hopes among American Negroes for integration into organized baseball" (61).

blacks but ended in violence, aided by the US Marines, cost the Avelars their property and Luis his Cuban baseball career; and that, of all the baseball relics that prompted the time travel of his mind, the one he treasured most and held aloft to his admirers was the carved, wooded statue created by young Luis.

Fulfilling Hopes and Dreams:
The Role of Religion in *Havana Heat*

The theme of religion in this novel is developed slowly but powerfully. In addition to providing colorful quotes and memorable characters, it also furnishes important information about American and Cuban history and culture, which adds another dimension to the novel.[5] Most of all, religion creates a dynamic that helps resolve the key issues of Dummy Taylor's dreams and Luis's need to become a man.

In the first part, Taylor makes a few passing references to his nominal Christian faith—some critical of the clergy and deacons, in the fashion of W. P. Kinsella. Dummy is a less than enthusiastic churchgoer, but he does attend a deaf church at the behest of his wife, Della. Taylor also uses religious terminology, as we have seen in earlier works, to express the hold that baseball has on people. When he was a child, "Comiskey's Browns had seemed like gods to me" (35); as an adult he was awed by his first glimpse of the Philadelphia Athletics' Shibe Park: "I'd expected something factory-like, but what rose before me seemed more a cathedral" (34).[6] He also

---

[5] Darryl Brock lists as one of his prime sources for cultural background on Cuba Hugh Thomas's book, *Cuba. The Pursuit of Freedom*. I will cite Thomas, Anthony B. Pinn, and Miguel Barnet to elaborate on the spiritual phenomena of *santería* that are so central to the novel.

[6] The ballpark as cathedral was celebrated in a landmark book called *Green Cathedrals*. It describes a feature of Shibe Park as a "French Renaissance church-like dome on exterior roof behind the plate" (70).

recalls that the Giants' black World Series uniforms made them appear as "angels of death" (11).

Once the story shifts to Cuba, it alternately features, in five sequences, the two major religions of the island, Roman Catholicism and *santería*. The players are first introduced to the latter on a tour of Havana.

> Red scarves were tied around the gigantic [ceiba tree[7]] trunk, and at the base were piles of pennies, fruits, and rum-soaked cakes. The guide explained that they were offerings to various gods, and that many more were buried between the protruding roots. Several chicken heads and a scary-looking black doll hung from the branches. "Gods?" said one of the Catholic players. "You mean saints?" "*Sí*," the guide said. "*Santos.*" (109-10)

As the role of *santería* emerges in the novel, Brock furnishes more explanation of it. Initially, however, we settle for the manager's gruff interpretation: "'It's voodoo, you bonehead,' McGraw said. 'Brought in from Africa by the slaves. Those things are blessings and hexes'" (110).

Indeed, the folk practices derive from the religion of the Yorùbás, a large West African ethnic group, many of whom were brought to Cuba by slave traders from the 1500s on. Although the slaves were nominally converted to Catholicism, they succeeded in maintaining the African tradition by displaying representations of their anthropomorphic deities (*orishas*) such as dolls, colors, numbers, drum and dance features, and favorite foods. The Yorùbás also adapted the *orishas* to the prevailing Catholic culture by

---

[7] The kind of tree is significant, for it is believed to be home to a major spirit and saint in the novel: "Changó, god of war, and St. Barbara remained an uneasy identification, living in a ceiba tree..., dressed alternately as a man and woman" (Thomas 1125). The androgynous nature of St. Barbara/Changó, also cited by Barnet (91), is shown by Brock in his depiction of Natalia.

clothing them in the favored costumes of Catholic saints. The syncretism of these two religions, with other African and indigenous influences, produced what is called *santería* (the way of the saints, or saint worship).[8]

On the same city tour, Dummy Taylor is approached by a shoeshine man claiming to be a *brujo* (witch) who, for one dollar, will give him a prediction from Taylor's *muerto* (protective spirit). Against the advice of a spooked teammate, Taylor plays along, curious why he was singled out. When the *brujo*, through the tour guide, tells him, "you will give birth while you are here.... He says it will be a boy" (111), Taylor assumes he has been had and moves on. Only later does he recall the incident as the first step in the spiritual process that will redefine his dream, point him to the first of his surrogate sons, and give him hope.

The Catholic presence in Cuba is represented above all by Padre Cipriano, called Father C., a priest who brings several deaf youngsters to the ballpark to root for Taylor. He wants Taylor to come to his city of Matanzas to work with and encourage the boys, one in particular, Luis Avelar. Realizing that this would require the team's permission, the priest obtains Manager McGraw's consent, with the proviso that Taylor can scout a sure pro prospect for the Giants.

Once in Matanzas, Taylor learns that his mission is also a spiritual one. "What I am truly interested in," explains Father C., "is Luis's *soul*. Once he was a loving boy, a bright spirit. Now he is on the way to...I don't know what. I fear for him" (197). Violently persecuted by hearing boys, Luis reacts by throwing fits, which gives rise to the charge that he is possessed by

---

[8] Pinn 68. Pinn also includes in his discussion of *santería* a helpful chart (73) outlining the direct correspondence of several *santería* divinities to Catholic saints. It lists the Yorùbá and *santería* names of the deity, the name of the equivalent saint, the functions of the deity/saint, and the colors associated with them. The anthology in which Barnet's article appears, *Sacred Possessions*, contains a helpful glossary of terms (283-88).

demons. Taylor is horrified: "Deaf kids were commonly seen as retarded or even crazy, but possessed by demons? Not in these times. Not in the U.S., anyway. But who knew about Cuba?" (197). Recalling those who encouraged and nurtured him, Dummy is willing to help.

At the tryout, where Luis faces his main antagonist, a powerful batter named Nico Santellán, a brawl erupts in which Taylor is clubbed senseless by a bat. When he awakes in the care of Luis's mother Natalia and sister Luna, the spiritual emphasis switches back to the Cuban folk religion. The *bohío* (hut) in which he lies contains accoutrements of *santería* that remind him of the shrine tree in Havana: "candles burned again, flanked now by black statues and coins shining in the flickering light. Something birdlike hung from the ceiling.... A pungent odor rose from a brass bowl behind the candles" (214). As Natalia mixes and applies a coconut paste to Taylor's wounded head, the player drifts off, be it in a spiritual or pathological reverie: "Time seemed to melt away. I entered a floating space where I hovered effortlessly.... I tried to look up and see her face. Her scarf was off, her hair a halo of snakes[9] backlit by the candles like a Medusa statue I'd once seen. Hardly a comforting vision, yet I felt oddly safe and protected" (214).

In the morning, the swelling on Taylor's head wound has subsided, and the pain in his pitching arm is gone. When Natalia ceremoniously buries the remaining healing paste beneath a palm tree, Taylor learns that she is *una santera*, a priestess selected by a particular deity and initiated into lifelong service after being "reborn *en santo*, in the spirit" (Pinn 70). Natalia further treats him with "a bucket of river water and scooped some out into a shell decorated with bits of yellow glass" (215), and she uses a chicken egg pur-

---

[9] The snake motif is reinforced on the next page when Natalia's large pet snake appears and terrifies Taylor. It also recalls both *The Seventh Babe* and *The Iowa Baseball Confederacy*, where root and snake imagery entwines the baseball action.

portedly to cleanse his body of poisons. She also expresses her gratitude for Taylor's concern for Luis, leaving the Giant hurler with "a family feeling"[10] and "thoroughly at peace" (217). Before Taylor's return to Havana, Father C. confirms Natalia's reputation as a healer and adds one more detail to the spiritual mysteries surrounding her family. Luis's enemies, he reports, "say that Luis is a monster and that he was deaf at birth because Natalia mated with demons who dwell in the trees[11] on her property" (218). Thus, we learn that the antagonism the padre wishes to overcome reflects not only bias against the deaf but also vicious gossip and superstition.

When Taylor later asks, "What would it take to make them all friends? …Can't you just give orders to their families?" (234), Father C. shrugs and explains that the Catholic Church is not as powerful in Cuba as elsewhere. He explains why in a pithy historical summary that recapitulates several events introduced by Brock in the course of the novel: "Well, it didn't help that José Martí was excommunicated. Or that the *reconcentrado* tragedy[12] went unopposed. During the struggle for independence a great deal of our land was lost, and then U.S. occupation brought separation of church and state. Civil marriage is now permitted, so people needn't come to us for that sacrament any longer…. And of course there is s*antería*" (234-35).

Before the big game, the priest, perhaps with "a hint of envy" (235), suggests that in Cuba "baseball works miracles" (235), and after the youth team defeats the Giants, he proclaims the victory "a miracle" (282). But the

---

[10] The idea of family is prominent in *santería*; allegiance to a particular *orisha* is determined paternally (Barnet 82).

[11] The basis for this rumor (besides pure malice) is the belief that the venerated deity Changó's "refuge, throne, and vantage point is the royal palm" (Barnet 91). We recall that Natalia chose to bury her excess coconut paste beneath a palm tree.

[12] In the 1890s the Spaniards, fighting insurgents, herded rural Cubans into fortified zones, in effect concentration camps. As Brock reports, between 200,000 and 450,000 people died of starvation and sickness.

miracle consists of more than a huge athletic upset. It resides in the boys' acceptance of Luis, growing inning by inning, as he gallantly shuts out the Giants, and in "Luis's becoming a man" (283). In the final, bizarre segment of the interior narrative, Taylor records yet one more miracle, two more prophecies, and not a little mystery.

To celebrate his role in Luis's development, Taylor is invited to a festival at the family's *bohío* in Matanzas. After the meal, Father C., sitting before Natalia's altar, reveals a second prophecy (the first being that of the shoeshine man), which was given at the recent feast of Saint Barbara: "a David would arrive—as in the story of Goliath—and be silent in his triumph" (291). The prophecy, however, comes not from a Catholic, but from a local *santero*, perhaps from Natalia. It appeared to have been fulfilled in Luis, who defeated the mighty Giants, or in another silent one, his mentor, Dummy, a prospect that gives Taylor "the willies" (291).

After saying a Mass for the Dead, Father C. retires for the evening. "The next part is not for me" (292), he states. He cannot appear to condone *santería* by remaining. What follows the Mass is Natalia's elaborate ritual, the fifth and decisive religious passage in the Cuban part of the novel. Taylor describes the various costumes, foods, and dancing, though he does not understand their significance. He wants to leave the alien ceremony, but the potent drink he swallows renders him powerless. A big, entranced dancer, possessed by the *orisha* Changó, approaches Taylor, massages his head,[13] and laughs loudly. "And I heard laughter," the deaf ballplayer writes. "*Heard it!*" (294). A miracle. He also sees the dancer's features transformed into those of Luis's grandfather, and back again.

---

[13] The head massage administered first to the ailing Taylor by Natalia and then by the dancer is part of the process of possession. "The god descends on the head of his *omó* (child), holding him prey to his most absolute will, forcing him to act involuntarily" (Barnet 86).

When released at last, Taylor stumbles outside to the mysterious palm grove and holds on while a lightning bolt strikes nearby and a rainstorm drenches the trees. In his deep drowsiness, he feels Natalia—who herself morphs into Luna and back—mount[14] him and "demand" his seed. "And then the stars all seemed to rush together and I felt myself slip over the edge of somewhere I'd never been" (296).[15]

The next morning, an addled Taylor wants to believe he was dreaming or simply overpowered and deluded by the strong drink, but author Brock provides no assurance that this is so. Instead, he hints that the power of *santería* has prevailed and what happened was "real." Taylor encounters evidence that points to a sexual experience under the palms, but is embarrassed to ask Natalia about it. Several details in Father C.'s explanation of the festival ritual[16] and a curious note from Natalia—"*Your seed will attract other sons*" (298)—appear to furnish the final pieces to the prophecy puzzle. The predictions of Taylor giving birth to a son and of a silent David

[14] Another aspect of possession is "mounting." It enables the spirit to return to earth in one of his descendants. "A possessed is a person who receives a god; the god mounts his 'horse'—that is, the person's body—and forces him into contortions and gestures that characterize the deity" (Barnet 86).

[15] Indeed, Taylor has never been there, namely deep in the erotic and spiritual grasp of *santería*, "chosen" by Ochún. While he does not become an initiate, possessed by and devoted for life to the *orisha*, he is profoundly affected by its power.

[16] The priest explains the distinctive trait of *santería*, the blend of Catholic saints and African deities, as it is manifested at Natalia's altar. "At midnight during festivals they often change from one to the other. La Caridad [Our Lady of Charity], for example, becomes Ochún, a peaceful, loving god. It is Ochún whom Natalia serves. Santa Bárbara, whose feast was this month, becomes Changó, the warrior god of fire and thunder.... Ochún is a soothing presence whose medium is water—the opposite of Changó, you see? Cooling and healing. Quenching the fire" (298).

Taylor sees that this information corresponds to his experience. He had described the liquor as a "river of fire" (293), and, of course, had witnessed the lightning in the palms, when "It smelled like the air itself was on fire" (295). The downpour that follows is "Natalia in the rain. Quenching the fire" (298). Thus, rather than a common drunken stupor, his swoon must be part of a cultic rite. We recall that Taylor, against his teammate's advice, had opened himself up to the magic of *santería* on the city tour, then submitted to its healing power after suffering the head injury. Finally, at the festival, he takes the intoxicating drink and yields to the *santería* deities. His erotic experience under the palms may be a spiritual reverie in the thrall of the *orishas*, but with no one else present. Or, just as the dancer, possessed by Changó, physically interacts with Taylor, perhaps Natalia, possessed by Ochún, forces herself on the American. Whether physically or spiritually, literally or figuratively, she wishes to receive his seed to produce more sons in fulfillment of her prophecy.

defeating Goliath had both been issued before the Giants' pitcher met Luis, and both prophecies are fulfilled in what can be called miraculous ways, through the ministrations of the Catholic Padre Cipriano and the *santera* Natalia. If Luis is the first son, then, according to Natalia's prophecy, others will follow—"attracted," not "produced," by the childless Taylor—as indeed they are in Dummy's long and fulfilling coaching career.

This is Taylor's final recollection on the novel's last page as he acknowledges his admirers at the awards ceremony. Content with his life that attracted many sons, holding the carved ballplayer statue aloft, he communes in spirit with his Cuban progeny: "Luis's fingers spoke to him and he answered back, their combined excitations so powerful it seemed that they must reach across the years and even to heaven" (304).

Conclusion:

This literary study asserts that, contrary to popular notions, baseball and fiction about baseball can be the object of serious academic inquiry. Both the game and its literature have a remarkable affinity for religious expression, and we chose this affinity as the subject of our inquiry. Three often distinct spheres—baseball, religion, and adult fiction—overlap, the result being a solid body of literature that greatly informs our understanding of modern American culture.

The national pastime is a key component of the national myth, the American dream, "the one constant through all the years" (*Shoeless Joe* 213), linking past with present, rural with urban, play with work, individual with team. It is also a glue that, despite certain friction, acculturates immigrant boys, creates affinities to other cultures, and binds together families.

The game itself, and Americans' devotion to it, possesses a magical, even religious quality. "Name me a more perfect game!" exclaims Kinsella's Matthew Clarke. "Name me a game with more possibilities for magic,

voodoo, hoodoo, enchantment, obsession, possession…. Abner Doubleday, if he did indeed invent the game, must have received divine guidance" (*IBC* 44). The game, it turns out, does possess an extraordinarily ritualistic quality. Baseball is defined by its rites and rules, temples and shrines, saints and sinners, relics and sacred texts, high priests and holidays.

Not surprisingly, the cultural interaction of baseball and religion, and the game's dual role as national pastime and civic religion, eventually captured the imagination of America's literati. This produced a distinctive subgenre within the excellent, if underrated, body of adult baseball fiction that emerged in the latter half of the twentieth century. The best of that fiction far transcended the formulaic tales marketed to young readers, offering more balanced portrayals of human existence, and richer, more critical perspectives of American history, society, and culture. Baseball novels featuring religion likewise create broader views of the American experience, with special emphasis on the religious character of the nation and the perceived (real or imagined) spiritual qualities of the game of baseball. The authors and the religions they portray cover a wide spectrum. They are atheists, parodists, searchers, and believers. Their big tent of religions covers Judaism, Catholicism, Protestantism, Adventism, Buddhism, Native American veneration of nature, and African-Caribbean-North American spiritism.

We find distinctive narrative structures that challenge us as readers and enrich the texts as we "decode" them. These novels and others are possessed of an overarching tension that goes far beyond the standard "Who will win the big game?" concern of earlier fiction. Can Joe Hardy and Sister Timothy save their souls and defeat the Devil? Can Babe Ragland find peace and an identity in baseball and voodoo? Does Ray Kinsella correctly interpret the messages that come to him from beyond, and can he save his farm? Will Drifting Away and Gideon Clarke succeed in their competing quests?

The most prevalent style of writing that we encountered was some form of magical realism, whose leading practitioner is the great Colombian novelist, Gabriel García Márquez. Magical realism lends itself well to a game distinguished by its appeal to our imagination, a tradition of youthful and middle-aged dreamers, and decades of lore. If the game itself has magical qualities, and novelists feature colorful wizards and root doctors, then magical realism is a most logical choice of style, creating the seamless correspondence of form and content that distinguishes great literature.

Beyond the academic hypotheses about the compatibility of baseball, literature, and religion, my fascination with this topic and zeal for sharing with my readers the depth and charm of the writings holds true. My expectations for researching this book were exceeded as I found ever more examples of the baseball-religion mix in American literature and culture, from the finest novels, analyzed in the preceding chapters, to the colorful speech and cultural artifacts documented in the appendix. Whether I have succeeded as an "evangelist" for baseball fiction—preaching baseball to readers and literature to baseball fans—will be determined by my readers. I should be delighted if this book were to bring them closer to the ideal "6" on the fan rating scale, and most gratified if they were prompted to *read*, not just read *about*, the splendid novels featured in this study.

Extra Innings: Appendix

I. Thumbnail Sketches of Other Works with Baseball and Religion

These works all have references to religion, some more directly or extensively than others, but for various reasons they do not get a place in the starting lineup of this study. The selection is based less on reputation and critical acclaim than on these three factors: (1) my interest in and ability to relate to the story and thus make it come alive for my readers; (2) the amount of material the work devotes to my specific topic: I don't wish to create a chapter so small that it would be out of proportion to the others; (3) the existing secondary literature on the work: too much would result in more rehash and less room for original commentary on my part. Of the works I discuss, only *Shoeless Joe* is the subject of an overwhelming number of critical pieces.

This list is not exhaustive. It is intended to provide additional literary and historical context to the nine novels discussed in individual chapters and to suggest more material that might be of interest to the reader.

Frank O'Rourke, "The Heavenly World Series" (1952; 2002). This story furnishes the title to a collection of O'Rourke short stories, nine in the original edition and eighteen in the reissue. In the featured story, deceased all-stars begin a series in heaven to determine which league is superior, the National or the American.

Robert Coover, *The Universal Baseball Association, Inc., J. Henry Waugh, Prop.* (1968). Coover's novel, a major work of the 1960s, depicts the alienation and obsession of an accountant who creates and is consumed by his own tabletop dice baseball league. The creator is J. Henry Waugh; with a little imagination the name is an echo of Jehovah. (Aside: One of my Wright State colleagues, when asked to join a fantasy league, refused, citing this book as a nightmare warning against obsession with baseball.)

Philip Roth, *The Great American Novel* (1973). An old sportswriter writes about a forgotten baseball league (cf. Kinsella's *IBC*) and its incredibly inept cellar-dwellers, the Ruppert Mundys. This is not a spiritual novel, but its heavy parody and satire uses numerous religious names and wordplays.

W. P. Kinsella, "The Last Pennant Before Armageddon" (1984). Al "The Hun" Tiller, manager of the Chicago Cubs, is not a religious man, but when God and an archangel inform him that "when the Cubs next win the National League Championship, it will be the last pennant before Armageddon," his managerial decisions assume apocalyptic proportions.

As the superpowers slide toward World War Three and the Cubs are one playoff game away from the pennant, Al weighs the calls of love and honor.

W. P. Kinsella, "The Battery," (1984). Dominican twin brothers begin playing catch in their mother's womb and eventually develop into Major Leaguers. The most colorful figure is a wizard who revels in prophecy, magic, bookmaking, and politics. Perhaps none of Kinsella's magical realism so exudes the energy of García Márquez (and Charyn) as this piece. Its portrayal of a phenom with the Washington Senators, coveted by the Yankees, recalls *The Year the Yankees Lost the Pennant.*

Frederick Manfred, *No Fun on Sunday* (1990). Another lesser-known novel that weaves baseball with rural family life is *No Fun on Sunday*. It celebrates the roots of baseball on sandlots and pastures and chronicles the life of a plains family torn between love for baseball and observance of the Sabbath.

David Craig, *Our Lady of the Outfield* (1999). A Catholic novel about the growing faith of a young professional ballplayer named Keith Wells. A devotional text, it stresses the role of Mary in sports and in everyday life.

Scoreboard watching

Florida Marlins center fielder Juan Pierre crashes into the Fenway Park scoreboard in an effort to haul in a fly ball of the bat of Boston's Bill Mueller. The Red Sox won, 11-7.

David Petreman found hidden meaning in this photo at Fenway Park's scoreboard. The final letters of each line are D-A-M-N-Y. The Y is part of NYY, New York Yankees, "damn Yankees." If the photo were from a New York game, one could stretch the analogy to see the outfielder as yet another opponent "crucified" by the Yankee juggernaut.

SABR convention convenes where baseball is a religion

To headline writers, faithful members of SABR (Society for American Baseball Research) qualify as religious devotees.

Fairhaven, like several churches, uses baseball to describe the path to greater involvement in the Christian life.

This stained-glass tribute to baseball is found in the "Sports Window" in New York's Cathedral of St. John the Divine.

This 1909 cartoon shows that even a century ago, devotion to baseball often assumed a religious quality.

This statue is one of several sports figurines marketed by Devon Trading and Catholicshopper.com.

Michael Langenstein's "Play Ball" suggests the divine origin of baseball.

All-Religious-Name Baseball Club

C—STEVE CHRISTMAS

1B—LUKE EASTER

2B—JOHNNY TEMPLE

3B—TIM TEUFEL (TEUFEL=DEVIL, GERMAN)

SS—JOSE PAGAN

OF—JESUS ALOU

OF—ANGEL BRAVO

OF—BOB CHRISTIAN

P—PREACHER ROE

P—JIM GOTT (GOTT=GOD, GERMAN)

P—BUBBA CHURCH

P—EDDIE PRIEST

MANAGER—HARRY LORD

GENERAL MANAGER—BRANCH RICKEY (BRANCH=O.T. MESSIAN-IC TITLE)

CHAPLAIN—BILLY SUNDAY

Baseball in the Bible

Most of this list originally appeared in a New York publication called *World-Over* and has been modified only slightly.

Opening Day: "In the big inning, God created the heavens and the earth." (*not* Genesis 1:1)

The lineup: "Every man of the Children of Israel shall pitch by their fathers' houses; every man with his own standard." (Numbers 2:2)

The miscue: "Who can understand errors?" (Psalm 19:13)

The fly ball: "He sent many flies among them and they caught every one!" (Psalm 78:45; 2 Samuel 2:15)

The bunt: "Amon sacrificed and Noah went in." (2 Chronicles 33:23; Genesis 7:7)

The player's girlfriend: "Rebekah came out with her pitcher." (Genesis 24:15)

The visiting team: "Then the Philistines went up and pitched in Judah." (Judges 15:19)

The frustrated manager: "Do I need madmen, that only have brought this fellow to play?" (1 Samuel 21:16)

The steal sign: "They ran as soon as he had stretched out his hand." (Joshua 8:19)

The game-winning home run: "And Absalom went in for a homer and Obner was beaten." (2 Samuel 16:22; 2:17; Hosea 3:2)

The unrelenting umpire: "And all the people shouted with a great shout. Whether it be good or bad, he shall not alter it." (Ezra 3:11; Leviticus 27:10, 12)

Two Tall Tales

Two old-timers, longtime friends and baseball fans, agree that the first to die will return to tell the other if there is baseball in heaven. After the one passes away, sure enough he floats back to report to his pal. "I've got good news and bad news," he says. "The good news is: there *is* baseball in heaven. The bad news is: you're pitching Wednesday."

On a hot day in hell, the Devil is threatening to turn up the heat. "Doesn't bother me," says one tough guy from Chicago. "I love the heat." The Devil cranks it up some more, but the guy just seems to thrive on it. "I'll fix you, wise guy," says the Devil and turns on the cooling system till the temperature falls below 32 degrees. "How's that, Mr. I-love-the-heat?" "Well, it is a bit chilly, but I couldn't be happier. It means the Cubs just won the World Series."

Quiz on "Religion as Baseball"

This quiz will test your knowledge of baseball and religious terminology and stimulate your sense for word plays. It's enjoyable, but some of them are a stretch, so don't get wrapped around the theological axle…and please don't take offense. It's all in fun! Fill in the blanks with the words listed below. The correct answers are given on page 182.

Lutherans, Preterists, Unitarians, Amillennialists, Amish, Premillennialists, Calvinists, Pagans, Methodists, Evangelicals, Atheists, Baptists, Adventists, Quakers, Pope, Episcopalians, Fundamentalists, Televangelists, Dunkers, Postmillennialists

---

1. _____ believe the game is fixed.

2. _____ believe they can't win, but trust the Scorekeeper.

3. _____ won't swing the bat.

4. _____ can catch anything, but can't find the right ballpark.

5. The _____ walk a lot.

6. _____ sacrifice.

7. _____ get traded every two years.

8. _____ get caught stealing.

9. _____ pass the plate.

10. _____ make effective pitches.

11. _____ balk.

12. _____ already know the final score.

13. The _____ never commits an error.

14. _____ are down by three.

15. _____ have a seventh-inning stretch.

16. _____ refuse to have an Umpire.

17. _____ want to play hardball.

18. _____ expect the game to be called soon on account of darkness.

19. _____ keep looking for the game to finally be perfected.

20. _____ just keep on playing and playing and playing.

Quotable Quotes

I count the loves in my life: Annie, Karin, Iowa, Baseball. The great god Baseball. —Ray Kinsella in W. P. Kinsella's *Shoeless Joe*

In the big inning, God created heaven and earth. —*Not* Genesis 1:1

If I were not a Christian, I would worship baseball. —The Rev. Dr. Greg Anderson

The Argentine writer Jorge Luis Borges said that to fall in love is to create a religion with a fallible god, and I had been worshiping at this shrine since I was ten. —Luke Salisbury

Baseball is more than a game to me—it's a religion. —Hall of Fame umpire Bill Klem

When I think of a stadium, it's like a temple. It's religious. —Jim Lefebvre

Baseball is like church—many attend but few understand. —Wes Westrum

A ballpark at night is more like a church than a church. —Ray Kinsella in W. P. Kinsella's *Shoeless Joe*

I believe in the church of baseball. I've tried all the major religions and most of the minor ones.... I've tried 'em all, I really have, and the only church that truly feeds the soul, day in, day out, is the church of baseball. —Susan Sarandon as Annie Savoy in the film *Bull Durham*

While the game's woes have been multiplying over the last few years, there has arisen, almost as a form of denial, a passionate romance for baseball in the

abstract—a fervid belief that in this game resides a beauty, a truth, a poetry, an Americanness of spirit and values. One might call it the Platonic form of baseball or the Church of Baseball because it floats above the particulars of the game in a state of exalted holiness. —Neal Gabler

Baseball was a kind of secular church that reached into every class and region of the nation and bound millions upon millions of us together in common concerns, loyalties, rituals, enthusiasms, and antagonisms. —Philip Roth

It's like my Garden of Eden in the middle of life. —Cleveland fan John Adams

Jesus can't, he's busy playing baseball with his friend Grandpa. —Samuel Merillat, age three and a half, whose grandfather had just died, explaining why Jesus couldn't sit with him at the moment

Baseball, like love and religion, should be taken on faith; its appeal is a mystery to be savored, not solved. —Bernard Ohanian

This is not only business. It's millions who truly love the game as a religion. —player agent Tom Reich

Next to religion, baseball has furnished a greater impact on American life than any other institution. —Herbert Hoover

I believe the designated hitter is a device of the Devil. —Hal McCoy, *Dayton Daily News* & Hall of Fame sportswriter

Answers to Quiz

1. Calvinists believe the game is fixed.

2. Lutherans believe they can't win, but trust the Scorekeeper.

3. Quakers won't swing the bat.

4. Unitarians can catch anything, but can't find the right ballpark.

5. The Amish walk a lot.

6. Pagans sacrifice.

7. Methodists get traded every two years.

8. Televangelists get caught stealing.

9. Episcopalians pass the plate.

10. Evangelicals make effective pitches.

11. Fundamentalists balk.

12. Preterists already know the final score.

13. The Pope never commits an error.

14. Dunkers are down by three.

15. Adventists have a seventh-inning stretch.

16. Atheists refuse to have an Umpire.

17. Baptists want to play hardball.

18. Premillennialists expect the game to be called soon on account of darkness.

19. Postmillennialists keep looking for the game to finally be perfected.

20. Amillennialists just keep on playing and playing and playing.

Works Cited

Aitken, Brian. "Baseball as Sacred Doorway." *Aethlon* 8/1 (Fall 1990): 61-75.

Albanese, Catherine. *America, Religions and Religion*. Belmont CA: Wadsworth Publishing Company, 1981.

Barnet, Miguel. "La Regla de Ocha: The Religious System of Santería." In *Sacred Possessions. Vodou, Santería, Obeah, and the Caribbean*, ed. Margarite Fernádez Olmos and Lizabeth Paravisini-Gebert, 79-100. New Brunswick NJ: Rutgers UP, 1997.

Barzun, Jacques. *God's Country and Mine*. NY: Vintage Books, 1954.

Beach, Charles Franklyn. "Joyful vs. Joyless Religion in W.P. Kinsella's *Shoeless Joe*." *Aethlon* 1611 (Fall 1998): 85-94.

Bjarkman, Peter C. "Introduction." In *Baseball & the Game of Life: Stories for the Thinking Fan*, ed. Peter Bjarkman. 9-21 Otisville,. New York: Birch Brook Press, 1990.

Boswell, Thomas. *How Life Imitates the World Series*. New York: Penguin, 1982.

———. "The Church of Baseball." In Geoffrey C. Ward, *Baseball: An Illustrated History*, 189-193. New York: Alfred A. Knopf, 1994.

Brock, Darryl. *Havana Heat*. New York: Penguin Putnam/Plume, 2000.

Candelaria, Cordelia. *Seeking the Perfect Game: Baseball in American Literature*. New York et al.: Greenwood Press, 1989.

Charyn, Jerome. *The Seventh Babe*. New York: Arbor House, 1979.

Chidester, David. "The Church of Baseball, the Fetish of Coca-Cola, and the Potlatch of Rock 'n' Roll." In *Religion and Popular Culture in America*, ed. Bruce David Forbes and Jeffrey H. Mahan, 219-238. Berkeley, Los Angeles, London: University of California Press, 2000.

Coover, Robert. *The Universal Baseball Association, Inc., J. Henry Waugh, Prop*. New York: Random House, 1968.

Craig, David. *Our Lady of the Outfield*. Oak Lawn IL: CMJ Marian Publisher, 1999.

Curtin, Kevin Thomas. "*The Natural:* Our *Iliad* and *Odyssey*." *The Antioch Review* 43/2 (Spring 1985): 225-41.

Dailey, Thomas F. "Believing in Baseball: The Religious Power of Our National Pastime." *Logos: A Journal of Catholic Thought and Culture* 6/2 (2003): 63-83.

Donohue, James F. *Spitballs & Holy Water.* New York: Avon, 1977.

Dostoevsky, Fyodor. *The Brothers Karamazov.* Trans. Constance Garnett. New York: The Modern Library, 1991.

Duncan, David James. *The Brothers K.* New York et al: Doubleday, 1992.

Easton, Rebecca. "*Shoeless Joe* as Allegory." *Aethlon* 17/1 (Fall 1999): 121-27.

Ellison, Ralph. *The Invisible Man.* NY: Random House, 1952.

Evans, Christopher H. and William R. Herzog II, editors. *The Faith of Fifty Million: Baseball, Religion, and American Culture.* Louisville: Westminster John Knox Press, 2002.

Faust. *The History of Doctor Johann Faustus.* Trans. H. G. Haile. Urbana: University of Illinois Press, 1965.

Fong, Bobby, "The Magic Cocktail: The Enduring Appeal of the 'Field of Dreams.'" *Aethlon* 11/1 (Fall 1993): 29-36.

Forbes, Bruce David and Jeffrey H. Mahan, editors. *Religion and Popular Culture in America*, 219-38. Berkeley, Los Angeles, London: University of California Press, 2000.

Frank, Margot. "Fyodor Dostoevsky." *Critical Survey of Long Fiction*, ed. Frank N. Magill, 503-17. Englewood Cliffs NJ: Salem Press, 1984.

"García Márquez, Gabriel." *Columbia Encyclopedia*, 5th edition, 1993.

García Márquez, Gabriel. *One Hundred Years of Solitude.* Trans. Gregory Rabassa. New York et al.: Harper & Row, 1970.

Gaughran, Richard. "The Hero as Outlaw: Jerome Charyn's *The Seventh Babe.*" *Elysian Fields Quarterly* 11/3 (1992): 90-96.

Giamatti, A. Bartlett. *Take Time for Paradise.* New York et al.: Summit Books, 1989.

Goethe, Johann Wolfgang. *Faust: Part One.* Trans. Bayard Taylor. Ed. Stuart Atkins. London: Collier Books, 1962.

Greenberg, Eric Rolfe. *The Celebrant.* New York: Penguin, 1986.

Grossinger, Richard, ed. *The Temple of Baseball.* Berkeley: North Atlantic Books, 1985.

Guthrie, Harvey H., Jr. "The Book of Ecclesiastes." *The Interpreter's One-Volume Commentary on the Bible.* Ed. Charles M. Laymon. Nashville and New York: Abingdon Press, 1971.

Hamblin, Robert, "Magic Realism, Or, The Split-Fingered Fastball of W. P. Kinsella." *Aethlon* 9/2 (Spring 1992): 1-10.

Healy, Dave and Paul Healy. "Half-Cultivated Fields: Symbolic Landscapes of Baseball." *Minneapolis Review of Baseball* 8 (Fall 1989): 31-37, 64.

Helterman, Jeffery. *Understanding Bernard Malamud.* Columbia: University of South Carolina Press, 1985.

Hershinow, Sheldon J. *Bernard Malamud.* New York: Frederick Ungar, 1980.

Holy Bible. New International Version. Grand Rapids: Zondervan Bible Publishers, 1973.

_____. King James Version.

Horvath, Brooke K. and William J. Palmer. "Three On: An Interview with David Carkeet, Mark Harris, and W. P. Kinsella." *MFS: Modern Fiction Studies* 33/1 (Spring 1987): 183-94.

Joffe, Linda S. "Praise Baseball. Amen. Religious Metaphors in *Shoeless Joe* and "Field of Dreams." *Aethlon* 7/2 (Spring 1992): 153-63.

Kahn, Roger. *The Boys of Summer.* New York et al.: Harper & Row, 1971.

Kinsella, W. P. "The Battery." In *The Thrill of the Grass.* Markham, Ontario et al.: Penguin, 1984.

———. *The Iowa Baseball Confederacy.* Toronto: Collins, 1986.

———. "The Last Pennant Before Armageddon." In *The Thrill of the Grass*, 3-21.

———. *Shoeless Joe.* New York: Houghton Mifflin, 1982.

Knapp, Liza. "The Brothers Karamazov by Fedor Dostoevskii." *Encyclopedia of the Novel.* Volume 1. Ed. Paul Schellinger. Chicago and London: Fitzroy Dearborn Publishers, 1998.

Lamberton, David and David James Duncan. "Meeting the Author of *The Brothers K.*" *Spectrum: Journal of the Association of Adventist Forums* 23/2 (August 1993): 31-35.

Land, Gary. "Adventism and the Church of Baseball." *Spectrum: Journal of the Association of Adventist Forums* 23/2 (August 1993): 27-30.

———. "Noncombatancy." In Gary Land, *Historical Dictionary of the Seventh-Day Adventists.* Lanham MD: Scarecrow Press, forthcoming.

Lauricella, John A. *Home Games. Essays on Baseball Fiction.* Jefferson NC; London: McFarland, 1999.

Lowry, Philip J. *Green Cathedrals.* Cooperstown NY: Society for American Baseball Research, 1986.

Malamud, Bernard. *The Natural.* New York: Farrar, Straus & Giroux, 1952.

Manfred, Frederick. *No Fun on Sunday.* Norman and London: University of Oklahoma Press, 1990.

McCleod, Nicole. "The Invisible Culture: Hoodoo in Georgia and South Carolina." <www.mamiwata.com/hoodoo2.html> (12 August 2003).

McCue, Andy. *Baseball by the Books.* Dubuque IA: Wm. C. Brown, 1991.

McGimpsey, David. *Imagining Baseball. America's Pastime and Popular Culture.* Bloomington: Indiana UP, 2000.

Michaud, Charles. Review of *The Brothers K* by David James Duncan. *Library Journal* 118 (1 June 1992): 172-73.

Morris, Timothy. *Making the Team: The Cultural Work of Baseball Fiction.* Urbana and Chicago: University of Illinois Press, 1997.

———. Online "Guide to Baseball Fiction": <www.uta.edu/english/tim/baseball/index.html>.

Mount, Nicholas J. "'Are the Green Fields Gone?: Pastoralism in the Baseball Novel." *Aethlon* 11/1 (Fall 1993): 61-77.

Murray, Don. *The Fiction of W. P. Kinsella. Tall Tales in Various Voices.* Fredericton New Brunswick: York Press, 1987.

Neihardt, John G. *Black Elk Speaks.* Lincoln and London: University of Nebraska Press, 1979.

O'Rourke, Frank. *The Heavenly World Series.* New York: A. S. Barnes, 1952; New York: Carroll & Graf, 2002.

Peterson, Richard. *Extra Innings: Writing on Baseball.* Urbana and Chicago: University of Illinois Press, 2001.

Peterson, Robert. *Only the Ball Was White.* New York et al.: McGraw Hill, 1970.

Pinn, Anthony B. *Varieties of African American Religious Experience.* Minneapolis: Fortress Press, 1998.

Podell, Tim. "Good Conversation!: A Conversation with Nancy Willard." Video recording. Scarborough NY: Tim Podell Productions, 1991.

Price, Joseph L. "Exit Laughing: The Eschatological Fusion of Now and Then, Here and There in 'Field of Dreams.'" Unpublished manuscript, 1990.

———. "The Pitcher's Mound as Cosmic Mountain: The Religious Significance of Baseball." In *From Season to Season: Sports as American Religion,* ed. Joseph Price, 61-76. Macon GA: Mercer UP, 2001.

Randall, Neil. "*Shoeless Joe*: Fantasy and the Humor of Fellow-Feeling." *MFS: Modern Fiction Studies* 33/1 (Spring 1987): 173-82.

Richman, Sidney. *Bernard Malamud.* New York: Twayne Publishers, 1966.

Ritter, Lawrence. *The Glory of Their Times.* New Enlarged Version. New York: Vintage Books, 1984.

Roth, Phillip. *The Great American Novel.* New York et al.: Holt, Rinehart and Winston, 1973.

Schwartz, Richard Alan. "Postmodernist Baseball." MFS: *Modern Fiction Studies* 33/1 (1987): 135-49.

Shannon, Mike. *Diamond Classics. Essays on 100 of the Best Baseball Books Ever Published.* Jefferson NC; London: McFarland, 1989.

_____. "The *Spitball* Interview: W. P. Kinsella." In *The Best of* Spitball*: the Literary Baseball Magazine,* ed. Mike Shannon, 52-69. New York: Pocket Books, 1988.

Solomon, Eric. "Counter-Ethnicity and the Jewish-Black Baseball Novel: The Cases of Jerome Charyn and Jay Neugeboren." MFS: *Modern Fiction Studies,* 33/1 (Spring 1987): 49-63.

Streng, Frederick J. *Understanding Religious Life,* 2nd edition. Encino CA; Belmont CA: Dickenson Publishing Co., 1976.

Thomas, Hugh. *Cuba. The Pursuit of Freedom.* New York et al: Harper & Row Publishers, 1971.

Tuten, Frederic. "Interview with Jerome Charyn." *Review of Contemporary Fiction* 12/2 (Summer 1992): 96-114.

Tygiel, Jules. *Past Time: Baseball as History.* Oxford; New York: Oxford UP, 2000.

Wallop, Douglass. *The Year the Yankees Lost the Pennant.* New York: W. W. Norton, 1954.

Westbrook, Deeanne. *Ground Rules. Baseball & Myth.* Urbana & Chicago: University of Illinois Press, 1996.

Wilder, Thornton. *Our Town,* in *Three Plays.* New York, Toronto, London: Bantam Books, 1966.

Willard, Nancy. *Telling Time: Angels, Ancestors, and Stories.* New York: Harcourt Brace & Company, 1993.

———. *Things Invisible to See.* New York: Alfred A. Knopf, 1984.

Williams, Raymond L. "Gabriel García Márquez," *Critical Survey of Long Fiction.* Foreign Language Series. Ed. Frank N. Magill. Englewood Cliffs NJ: Salem Press, 1984.

Aaron, 56, 57
Aitken, Brian, 60
Albanese, Catherine, 72
Almeida, Rafael, 155
American Indian folk religion, 108,
    114-20, 166
Anderson, Greg, 1, 3
Anderson, Sparky, 4
anti-Semitism, 81
Asinof, Eliot, 79
Baptists, 44, 128
Barnet, Miguel, 156, 160, 161, 162
Bartimaeus, 74
Barzun, Jacques, 13
Beach, Charles Franklin, 73
Bee, Clair, 2
Bennett, Eddie, 46
Bible, The, 31, 53, 54, 70, 74, 83, 113,
    114, 115, 139
Bjarkman, Peter C., 18
Black Elk, 114, 117, 120
Black Elk Speaks, 114
Black Sox scandal, 17, 61, 70, 78, 86
Boston Braves, 28
Boston Red Sox, 46, 49, 52, 55, 63
Boswell, Thomas, 9
Boys of Summer, The, 66
Bradbury, Ray, 61
Brautigan, Richard, 61, 69
Brock, Darryl, 31, 33, 46, 147-163
Brooklyn Dodgers, 24, 66
Brooks, Noah, 14
Brothers K, The, 12, 47, 127-46, 148
Brothers Karamazov, The, 129, 131,
    137-40
Broun, Heywood Hale, 15
Bruton, Bill, 42
Buddhism, 130, 136, 141
Bull Durham, 9
Cain, 103
Campbell, Joseph, 60

Candelaria, Cordelia, 18
Capone, Al, 34
Carkeet, David, 2
Celebrant, The, 11, 18, 77-88, 131, 148
Chadwick, Henry, 153
Charyn, Jerome, 33, 39, 45-58, 91, 171
Chicago American Giants, 34, 38
Chicago Cubs, 10, 60, 61, 108, 113, 116,
    170, 171
Chicago White Sox, 15, 17, 61, 65
Chidester, David, 9
Christianity, 1, 12, 16, 26, 43, 54, 102,
    104, 108, 113-14, 119, 156
Churchill, Winston, 142
Cincinnati Reds, 61, 87
Cleveland Indians, 11, 21
Coover, Robert, 170
Craig, David, 171
Curtin, Kevin Thomas, 18
Dailey, Thomas F., 9
Damn Yankees, 22
Darwin, Charles, 141, 142
Deloria, Vine, 115
Dickens, Charles, 137
Donlin, Mike, 148
Donne, John, 90
Donohue, James F., 4, 33-44
Dostoevsky, Fyodor, 137-140, 145
Doubleday, Abner, 70, 110, 166
Dream Team, The, 47
Duncan, David James, 12, 127-46
Durso, Joseph, 79
Duvall, Robert, 29
Easton, Rebecca, 60, 72
Eisenhower, Dwight, 22
Ellison, Ralph, 50
Esau, 93, 95
Evans, Christopher, 19
Faulkner, William, 47
Faust legend, 22, 25-27, 31, 111, 123
Fenway Park, 54, 55, 63

Field of Dreams, 60, 62, 72
Fitzgerald, F. Scott, 69
Fong, Bobby, 60
Foster, Rube, 38, 46
Frank, Margot, 138
Frazee, Harry, 47
Fullerton, Hugh, 85, 86, 87
Gaedel, Eddie, 29
García Márquez, Gabriel, 47, 48, 52, 61, 91, 93, 167, 171
Gaughran, Richard, 51, 52
Gehrig, Lou, 34, 38
Giamatti, A. Bartlett, 5, 11
Glory of Their Times, The, 2, 79
"Godfather Death," 91, 97
Goering, Hermann, 95, 97, 99
Goethe, Johann Wolfgang von, 26, 27, 98, 111
Goff, Bill, 10
Graham, Archibald "Moonlight", 44, 61, 63-67, 70, 72-74, 116
Great American Novel, The, 108
Great Gatsby, The, 69
Greenberg, Eric Rolfe, 2, 11, 31, 77-88
Grey, Zane, 2
Grimm, Jacob and Wilhelm, 91, 97
Gullah language, 101
Guthrie, Harvey H., Jr., 111
Haddix, Harvey, 42
Hall of Fame, 8, 9, 64, 71
Hamblin, Robert, 60
Harridge, Will, 29
Harris, Mark, 15, 20
Harvey, 61
Havana Heat, 37, 38, 41, 45, 49, 75, 91, 101, 127, 147-63
Healy, Dave and Paul, 68
Hemingway, Ernest, 18
Henry VIII, 77
Hershinow, Sheldon J., 18
Herzog, William R. II, 19

Homer, 17, 18
hoodoo, 57, 110, 166
Iliad, The, 18
Iowa Baseball Confederacy, The, 37, 39, 40, 42, 43, 46, 49, 54, 57, 61, 68, 77, 91, 92, 95, 107-25, 148, 159, 166, 170
Isaac, 94
Jackson, Joe, 17, 54, 61, 62, 65, 68, 69, 72, 75
Jacob, 93, 116
James, William, 47
Jesus Christ, 23, 24, 41, 73, 86-89, 99, 116, 118, 139, 145
Jewish baseball fiction, 20
Joan of Arc, 33, 34, 37, 38, 39, 43, 44
Job, 26, 30, 95
Joffe, Linda, 72
John the Baptist, 83
Judaism, 12, 80, 102, 166
Jung, C. G., 17
Kahn, Roger, 66-68
Kennedy, Bobby, 62
King David, 74
King Lear, 68
King Solomon, 74, 111
Kinsella, W. P., 2, 3, 4, 11, 12, 15, 18, 31, 33, 34, 35, 36, 37, 39, 40, 42, 43, 44, 53, 54, 59-76, 77, 92, 107-25, 128, 134, 135, 156, 165, 170, 171
Klem, Bill, 8, 9
Lamberton, David 127
Landis, Judge Kenesaw Mountain, 46, 50, 51, 54, 70, 72, 88
Lardner, Ring, 15
Lauricella, John, 18
Lazzeri, Tony, 34
Lloyd, John Henry "Pop", 36
Los Angeles Dodgers, 60
magical realism, 47, 48, 58, 60, 61, 90, 91, 101, 104
Malamud, Bernard, 15-18, 27-31, 34,

40, 41, 42
Manfred, Frederick, 171
Maris, Roger, 141, 142
Marsans, Armando, 155
Martí, José, 154, 160
Mary, 171
Maryland, University of 22
Mathewson, Christy, 77-88, 148
McCleod, Nicole, 57
McCue, Andy, 14, 33
McGimpsey, David, 18
McGinnity, Joe, 83, 84
McGraw, John, 78, 79, 80, 82, 83, 86,
    87, 147, 148, 151, 157, 158
Melville, Herman, 47
Merkle, Fred, 82
Michaud, Charles, 138
Miller, Richard L., 3
Moby Dick, 2
Morris, Timothy, 18
Moses, 23, 56, 73, 110
Mount, Nicholas J., 60
Nabokov, Vladimir, 47
Natural, The, 15-18, 27-31, 34, 40, 41,
    42, 46, 47, 81, 92, 119, 122
New York Giants, 78, 80, 83, 86, 147,
    148, 150, 153, 155, 157
New York Yankees, 21, 22, 23, 24, 25,
    28, 30, 34, 38, 46, 60, 171
Noah, 108
Odyssey, The, 18, 22, 68
One Flew Over the Cuckoo's Nest, 47
One Hundred Years of Solitude, 47, 48
Oppenheimer, J. Robert, 141, 142
O'Rourke, Frank, 170
Our Town, 63, 66
Paige, Satchel, 36
Patten, Gilbert, 14
Paul, 74
Peterson, Richard, 18
Peterson, Robert, 34, 36, 38, 155

Philadelphia Athletics, 150, 156
Pinn, Anthony B., 156, 158, 159
Polo Grounds, 63, 73, 78, 82, 84, 88
Popular Culture Association (PCA), 3
Portis, Charles, 37
Price, Joseph L., 9, 10, 72, 109
Protestantism, 12, 38, 44, 54, 148, 166
Randall, Neil, 64
rapture, 41, 54, 70, 71, 112, 117, 123
Richman, Sidney, 18
Ritter, Lawrence, 2, 79
Robinson, Frank, 38
Robinson, Henry Morton, 38
Roman Catholicism, 12, 33-44, 53, 148,
    157, 158, 160, 161, 162, 163, 166, 171
Roth, Philip, 108, 170
Rothstein, Arnold, 69
Russian Orthodoxy, 139
Ruth, Babe, 17, 34, 36, 37, 38, 41, 42,
    45, 46, 49, 51, 141
Saint Louis Browns, 47
Salinger, J. D., 37, 44, 54, 61-65, 67, 70,
    72, 73, 75, 112, 117, 152
santería, 41, 101, 148, 151, 157-63
Schwartz, Richard Alan, 60
Seaver, Tom, 5
Seventh Babe, The, 18, 39, 45-58, 60, 75,
    91, 100, 122, 148, 159
Seventh Day Adventism, 12, 128, 129,
    130, 139, 146, 166
Shakespeare, William, 77
Shannon, Mike, 19, 23, 31
Shelley, Percy, 89
Shibe Park, 156
Shoeless Joe, 3, 6, 11, 15, 37, 38, 43, 47,
    54, 58, 59-76, 77, 91, 110, 112, 116,
    117, 135, 148, 152, 165, 169
Smith, Al, 34, 35
Snodgrass, Fred, 86
Society for American Baseball Research
    (SABR), 3

Solomon, Eric, 18
spiritism, 12, 100-103, 166
Spitballs and Holy Water, 33-44, 46, 47,
    53, 61, 71, 91, 104, 119, 148
Sporting News, The, 9, 82
Stevens, Harry M., 82
Stratemeyer, Edward, 14
Streng, Frederick, 9, 109, 110
Take Time for Paradise, 11
Taylor, Luther "Dummy", 37, 41, 147-
    63
Temple of Baseball, The, 10
Things Invisible to See, 35, 38, 39, 43,
    45, 47, 50, 57, 66, 75, 89-106, 107,
    122, 127, 128
Thomas, Hugh, 156, 157
Tinker, Joe, 112
Tolkien, J. R. R., 64
Trinidad language, 101
Tunis, John, 14
Twain, Mark, 137
Tygiel, Jules, 3
Veeck, Bill, 29
voodoo, 45, 46, 48, 53, 55, 56, 58, 75,
    110, 148, 157, 166
Wagner, Honus, 36
Waitkus, Eddie, 17
Wallop, Douglass, 21-31, 63, 99
Washington Senators, 21, 22, 24, 25, 27,
    28, 171
Wasserman, Earl R., 18
Wayne, John, 37
Weaver, Earl, 8
Westbrook, Deeanne, 18, 22
Westrum, Wes, 6
Wheeler, John, 79, 84, 85
Whitman, Walt, 152
Wilder, Thornton, 66
Willard, Nancy, 4, 33, 39, 54, 75, 89-106
Williams, Raymond L., 48
Wizard of Oz, The, 61

World Series, 10, 24, 34, 61, 69, 71, 85,
    86, 87, 150, 154, 157, 170
Wovoka, 115
Wrigley Field, 10
Yankee Stadium, 10, 34, 44
Year the Yankees Lost the Pennant, The,
    21-31, 35, 46, 61, 91, 148, 171
Zeus, 123